FRESH WIND
OF THE SPIRIT

FRESH WIND OF THE SPIRIT

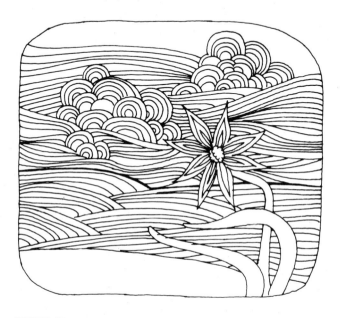

KENNETH CAIN KINGHORN

ABINGDON
NASHVILLE

FRESH WIND OF THE SPIRIT

Library of Congress Cataloging in Publication Data

KINGHORN, KENNETH C.
  Fresh wind of the Spirit.
  1. Holy Spirit.   I. Title.
BT121.2.K525   231'.3   74-7415

ISBN 0-687-13495-1

Scripture quotations unless otherwise noted are from the Revised Standard Version of the Bible, copyrighted 1946, 1952, and 1971 by the Division of Christian Education, National Council of Churches, and are used by permission.

Scripture quotations noted Phillips are from The New Testament in Modern English, copyright 1958 by J. B. Phillips.

Scripture quotations noted NEB are from The New English Bible. © the Delegates of the Oxford University Press and the Syndics of the Cambridge University Press 1961, 1970. Reprinted by permission.

Scripture quotations noted TEV are from the Today's English Version of the New Testament. Copyright © American Bible Society 1966.

Quotations noted TLB are from *The Living Bible,* copyright © 1971 Tyndale House Publishers, Wheaton, Illinois. Used by permission.

Manufactured by the Parthenon Press at
Nashville, Tennessee, United States of America

To

my students

past and present

Contents

Preface

The general religious renewal which flourishes today has produced a widespread interest in the Holy Spirit. Unfortunately, for many the work of the Holy Spirit is often veiled by a haze of confusion and ignorance. Failure to understand the working of the Holy Spirit has resulted in misplaced zeal, odd theological doctrines, and numbers of disappointed Christians.

The Christian church over the centuries has studied Scripture and hammered out a solid core of biblical teaching about the Holy Spirit, and this teaching can be of great value to the present spiritual revival. Of course the church has not settled all its theological problems, and it has made its share of mistakes. But in spite of its flaws, the church has an enormous treasury of biblical truth which is available to us today.

For some time I have felt the need for a book on the work of the Holy Spirit which takes into account both Scripture and the best thinking of the church. In writing such a book, I have tried to tread the middle way between heavy theology, which often presents technical barriers to the lay reader, and light devotional thoughts, which center almost exclusively in experience and sometimes neglect the mature conclusions of the great writers of the past.

So this book is a summary of my understanding of the work of the Holy Spirit, written for the layman and with a constant view to Scripture, orthodox theology, and the experience of other Christians. I have tried always to let Scripture be the final guideline in my conclusions.

Although this volume does not discuss every phase of the Spirit's operation, I have included what I believe to be the crucial issues relating to the work of God's Spirit in the life of the Christian believer. These pages were written especially for those who want to understand and experience what Jesus called *the* promise—the promise of the Holy Spirit.

KENNETH CAIN KINGHORN

I

What's Blowing in the Wind

This time,
like all times,
is a very good one,
if we but know
what to do with it.

—Ralph Waldo Emerson

The sun had set. The activities of the day were now history. Busy sounds of the marketplace had gradually given way to the softer night sounds of a city at rest. Winding his way along the narrow streets of the sleepy city, Nicodemus was on his way to seek an interview with Jesus.

Nicodemus recognized that Jesus was no ordinary teacher; he stood out above others as one who spoke with divine authority. Certainly, no one could do such miracles as Jesus had been doing unless God were with him.

Nicodemus didn't have to present an elaborate set of questions in order to draw Jesus into conversation. Sensing immediately his visitor's sincerity, Jesus launched into one of his most enlightening discourses. In the course of his teaching, Jesus compared the Holy Spirit's working to the wind: "You hear the sound of it," he said, "but you do not know whence it comes or whither it goes" (John 3:8). Although the source of the wind lies beyond human understanding, its effects can clearly be seen all around us.

To those with eyes to see and ears to hear, the wind of the Holy Spirit is blowing in significant ways in our own time. Signs are appearing on every hand that God is moving marvelously among us, producing a profoundly vital religious awakening—an awakening that holds promise of real hope for the future.

For one thing, the Spirit of God is helping us to see our need of something beyond ourselves. Modern man is increasingly admitting that he is unable to cope with the demands of daily life. The naïve optimism of a bygone religious humanism is rare today. Our culture is beginning to face realistically man's moral and spiritual dilemma, and people are refusing to settle for easy answers which offer no real hope. We want solutions that reach down to the root issues of life and offer meaning to us in the inner sanctuary of our souls.

Pleasure, material comforts, mysterious Eastern religious cults, and mind-expanding drugs have failed to satisfy our spiritual hunger. Man's failure to find meaning to life tells the story of his spiritual quandary, of his inability to produce convincing solutions to his spiritual questions. Surely, the Holy Spirit stands behind our growing spiritual hunger and our continuing quest for satisfaction. He is helping us to see our need for God.

But if contemporary man is recognizing his spiritual needs, he is also discovering God's remedy: through Jesus Christ individuals can be changed within and thereby find spiritual healing and spiritual satisfaction. Growing numbers are coming to know God personally as they become properly attuned to Jesus Christ. Thoughtful observers of the religious scene today are saying that spiritual renewal is the great new fact of our era.

Of course, this is not the first time that God's Spirit has brought fresh breezes to the church. He has also moved graciously in other times. In fact, the drama of man's religious history has regularly been characterized by periods of revival and spiritual vitality. By no means does this pattern suggest that God acts capriciously, arbitrarily sending us times of spiritual midnight and times of spiritual noonday. He always stands ready to bless mankind, but he can do so only as we recognize our need and turn to him.

Let's look at several instances of spiritual revival in other times.

The era of the kings in the Old Testament saw times of spiritual declension and times of spiritual renewal. Accordingly, God's people suffered periods of defeat and humiliation and periods of God's manifest blessing.

Again, the long centuries prior to Christ's birth were dark centuries. God seemed silent for a span of four hundred years. This age of spiritual dearth was followed by God's sending his Son in the Incarnation to bring us the revelation of the Christian gospel. The long period of darkness was followed by great light.

Then look at Acts! In that exciting book we read of Pentecost and of God's Spirit moving as a mighty wind, turning thousands from their own way to God's way. By the Spirit's power the early Christians turned the world upside down, and they developed the doctrinal foundations for the Christian church.

Another instance of the cycle of religious renewal was the great spiritual surge which erupted in the thirteenth century. The revival which flowered in those days expressed itself in the birth of the mendicant orders, particularly the Franciscans and the Dominicans. Inspired men left the silent monasteries, went out into the noisy streets, and taught and healed spiritually hungry people.

The wind of the Spirit moved once more in an especially vital way during the sixteenth century—the century of the Protestant Reformation. Tens of thousands of lives were changed as people experienced inwardly the reality of justification by faith.

Again in the eighteenth century God moved mightily. Pietism in Germany brought spiritual renewal to the Lutheran state church which had bogged down in a series of hostile theological disputes. In England, revival brought new life to many staid Anglican church members and gave birth to Methodism. At about the same time, the American colonies along the eastern coast of this country experienced a spiritual revival now known as the "First Great Awakening."

The second phase of this spiritual awakening shook America during the nineteenth century. This "Second Great Awakening" accompanied the westward move of the frontier population, and it became the means of bringing many to God. Several of the larger present-day denominations owe much of their earlier rapid growth to this significant spiritual revival.

All these times of spiritual quickening resulted from unusual outpourings of God's Spirit. Such times have been significant epochs in which history has been changed. Situations were altered for the better, and threatening cultural calamities were averted. God moved upon his people and sent a divine refreshing.

History shows that spiritual growth and advancement have come in spurts. We reach a plateau and tend to become dormant; then renewal comes, and we advance to a new plateau. Many sensitive Christians believe that history is repeating itself because God's Spirit is moving among us once again in an unusual way, renewing the church and offering a spiritual renaissance.

Of course, God never repeats in exactly the same way what he has done in the past. Although the *content* of revival is usually much the same, the *form* normally takes new shapes. The Franciscan movement and nineteenth-century revivalism ministered effectively to their respective generations. One suspects, however, that God has new and more relevant forms of ministry for today.

God can and does create new wineskins for the wine of the gospel. To seek to return to the "good old days" is not a wise strategy. For in doing so, we may fail to recognize the new things that the wind of God's Spirit is doing today.

Spiritual renewal, in the final analysis, never stems from resurrecting old forms or methods. Revival follows our obedience to Christ and our response to the moving of God's Spirit. Individual persons as well as religious institutions are renewed only by divine power.

In our day, two facts specifically stand out as evidence of God's working. These are the rise of an ecumenical spirit among Christians and the growth of lay involvement in the work of the church. Doubtless, future church historians will note these two phenomena—ecumenicity and lay aggressiveness—as two of the major developments of twentieth-century Christianity.

A new spirit of acceptance and cooperation is growing among contemporary Christians. In a new way, denominational prejudices and theological bigotry are thawing in response to the ministry of the Holy Spirit. To be ecumenical does not mean repudiating one's own denominational tradition, nor does it require hasty denominational mergers.

The ecumenical spirit at its best does mean, however, that a spirit of love and mutual trust among Christians replaces a spirit of selfish competition. Ecumenism means that Christians realize they have much more to agree upon than they have to quarrel about. In the face of the minority position of the Christian church and the enormity of the task ahead, Christ's followers are coming to see that they can ill afford to squabble over minor doctrinal and cultic differences. Moreover, contemporary Christians are discovering their common unity in Jesus Christ as Lord. The post-Reformation doctrinal disputes among Christians are yielding to a new mood of mutual giving and receiving. Even Roman Catholics and Protestants are surrendering many of their suspicions of each other, and new trust relationships are emerging. Love is replacing hate as Christians are taking seriously Paul's statements about the unity of the church (Gal. 3:28; Col. 3:11; Eph. 4:11, 12) and Christ's prayer that we may all be one (John 17:20, 21).

Also encouraging is the fact that lay people are no longer content to snuggle comfortably into the ship's hold and leave the direction of the ship to the clergy. They are starting to take their share of spiritual responsibility. Truly, God's "frozen people" are thawing out! Christian laymen are increasingly involved in the work of Christian ministry to the world around them. They are serving and bearing a Christian witness with a new dedication. The church is no longer exclusively a "clergymen's church," and this new development stands out as a very hopeful sign.

The growing ecumenical spirit among Christians and the rise of the laity hold enormous potential for the spiritual renewal we have been talking about. Both ecumenism and the lay awakening are twentieth-century phenomena, and they are occurring in the so-called mainline denominations. These developments are certainly not historical accidents. Surely God is preparing us for one of the greatest outpourings of renewal since Pentecost.

God, however, never forces spiritual revival upon us. Certain attitudes on our part are necessary before God can complete his gracious working in our lives. In order to benefit from the work of the Holy Spirit two basic attitudes are necessary: we must be *earnest* and we must be *receptive*.

First, we must be earnest if the Holy Spirit is to work fully in our lives. The Christian faith is more than entertaining ideas about God or knowing the doctrines of the Christian faith. It involves an inner passion to relate to God in a personal way. Christianity is intensely individual, and a true knowledge of God hinges upon our being sincere and earnest.

In matters such as science we may remain disinterested. Religion involves us at the deepest level of our being. When Christ confronts us, we can no longer remain spectators; we must become participants. If we remove the personal and emotional elements of religion, we have little left—as if we took these elements out of listening to a symphony, watching a sunset, or being married. The very nature of Christian faith requires personal, existential participation.

Centuries ago, God stressed to the Hebrew people the importance of being earnest. "You will seek me and find me; when you seek me with all your heart" (Jer. 29:13). God looks for the same attitude in us today.

A minister was talking with a girl in her early twenties: "I've looked for God," she said, "but I can't find him."

"Where did you look?" he asked.

"In church," she replied.

"That's a good place to begin," he said. "Tell me about it."

She said, "Well, for the first time in years I went to church, and during the service I prayed. I asked God to come closer to me so that in the future if I ever do get ready to become a Christian, he'll be around." She added, "But I can't find him."

The minister suggested, "Wasn't your prayer pretty

evasive? Perhaps God doesn't seem real because you haven't sought him sincerely." Then the minister asked, "Why not ask him right now to come into your life—all areas of it—and really mean it?"

For several moments she considered what he had said; then her face brightened as she replied, "Okay, I'll do it! I want to know God more than anything else, and I want to know him now."

As they prayed together, she entered into a firsthand relationship with Christ. When the two of them parted, she was radiant with Christian joy. Only when she put her whole self into her prayer did God meet her in a satisfying way.

God understands the difference between a halfhearted prayer and one that rises from the depths of our being. Having four children in our home, my wife and I have become experts in understanding the cries of infants. We have discovered that there are two types of cries which can arise in the middle of the night. We call them cry A and cry B.

Cry A occurs when the child stirs in his sleep and only whimpers slightly. The cry lacks enthusiasm and is not really an earnest cry. We do not respond to this sort of cry immediately because we know that the child is not very determined. He will soon go back to sleep.

But cry B is different. We've found that this sort of cry is totally sincere; it comes from the depths. When cry B begins we know that one of us might as well get up, because the child will probably not stop crying until he gets what he wants.

If parents can tell which cry shows real distress, then certainly God knows when we earnestly pray. He responds to every heartfelt prayer offered to him. God even welcomes our honest doubts; but in his sight halfhearted religion is worse than none at all.

God's Spirit gave to John a message for the church which remains applicable for us today: "I know your works: you are neither cold nor hot. Would that you were cold or hot! So, because you are lukewarm, and neither cold nor hot, I will spew you out of my mouth" (Rev. 3:15,16). A basic requirement for spiritual renewal is that we become earnest.

Second, we must be receptive if the Holy Spirit is to work fully in our lives. To be receptive means consciously to open one's self to the Spirit's working. God respects our freedom of choice; he never forces his will upon us. The Holy Spirit comes to those who show willingness to receive him.

Sometimes we develop a false confidence in our own ability to handle life's situations. So long as we feel self-sufficient, we are not likely to sense the need for the operation of the Holy Spirit in our lives. Smug Pharisees, who thank God that they have no spiritual needs, fail to demonstrate a receptivity to God's working. The Holy Spirit can work effectively in us only as we abandon our do-it-yourself religion.

God does not ask that we earn his favor, nor does he require that we become worthy to receive the presence of his Spirit. But he does require that we become willing —that we trust in his love and open ourselves to his healing grace. In short, he asks that we become as receptive as a little child.

One evening after an army chaplain had spoken to a group of soldiers preparing to depart for overseas, a burly corporal said, "I try hard to do right by everybody, yet I feel empty on the inside."

The chaplain answered, "Perhaps the Holy Spirit is trying to say something very important to you."

"What's that?" he asked.

"Maybe he's trying to say, 'Quit trying so hard to become spiritually adequate. Let *Christ* become your adequacy.' " The chaplain went on to say that God does not demand that we reach perfection or that we succeed in climbing a ladder to him. But he does ask us to allow him to reshape our lives by his indwelling presence.

So long as we seek to reach God through our own merit or to earn his favor through our own efforts, we will feel as empty as that corporal did. However, when we open ourselves to God's reaching out to us, we can benefit from the working of his Spirit. E. Stanley Jones summed up this concept in the phrase "Victory through surrender."

Perhaps God is saying to those of us who make up Christ's church today, "You have huge budgets, great buildings, ingenious programs. You do many wonderful works in Christ's name. These are good. But most of your activity is done without my help. Tarry and wait for the enabling of the Holy Spirit. Let me fill you with a liberating sense of my presence."

This much is certain: God's Spirit is moving among us today, offering new life and spiritual regeneration.

Even as God revived his people in other periods of history, he is doing a special work among us today. The promise of renewal is in the air.

As the movement of an ocean breeze defies analysis with respect to its source and its destination, so it is with God's Spirit. He is unpredictable; he is sovereign; he moves as he wills. And yet, he has promised to fill any life which is completely open to him.

Let me tell you a modern parable.

When I was nine years old, I heard an amazing theory. The older boys—about eleven and twelve years old—told my younger brother and me that if we planted chocolate candy wrappers we could grow candy bushes. But they had to be just the right type: brown, corrugated paper cups. We found some of these candy wrappers and planted them in Dad's garden. We tended them with great care. We staked them. We watered them. We weeded them. We even put barnyard fertilizer on them. All our efforts produced nothing. Not a single cup spouted into a candy bush!

Perhaps we of the church have listened more to the faulty advice of human traditions than we have to the biblical witness. We have sometimes tended to reduce the gospel to the doctrine of human endeavor. Little wonder some of our religious efforts have failed to produce the expected fruit. We have planted the candy wrappers of man's ingenuity and expected to reap a harvest of the Holy Spirit. Regardless of how hard we strive, we cannot produce the fruit of the Spirit without his working in our lives. Happily, the winds of renewal are changing our ideas!

In our own time, thousands of Christians are becoming vital, and thousands of non-Christians are coming to faith. The treetops of current history are stirring with the movement of the Spirit of God. And God is calling each one of us to participate in the mighty visitation of his Spirit in our day.

The Holy Spirit is seeking to permeate the consciousness of persons everywhere with his ministry of spiritual wholeness, new life, and creative love. Even now, God's offer extends to you. This, my friend, is what's blowing in the wind.

II

Are You Ready?

Unless there is within us that which is above us,
we shall soon yield to that which is about us.
—Peter Taylor Forsythe

The new life offered by Christ relates very definitely to the here and now. If we were to limit the power of the gospel to "going to heaven when we die," we would fail to grasp the full message of the New Testament. The abundant life mediated by the Holy Spirit touches all areas of our present existence.

In this chapter we'll think about what is initially involved in being "in Christ." But first, let's look at the basic reason why many persons fail to participate in the life of his Spirit. Our problem lies within ourselves. Let me illustrate.

One spring my three young sons and I began to stir up the rich earth in our family garden. We were all exhilarated by fresh air and warm April sun. One of the small boys begged me to let him try his hand at the power cultivator.

"Are you ready for this?" I asked.

"I'm ready, I'm ready!" he grinned.

I knew he could never make it alone, but he insisted.
I yielded.

His small hands reached only halfway around the handles, but with admirable confidence he started down the long row. However, in less than a yard's distance, he hit a snag. The machine lunged wildly. He had lost control. Hopelessly, he dropped his hands and shouted, "Help, Dad! I can't handle this thing!"

We're all like this at times, aren't we? When we try to take matters into our own hands, we botch things rather badly. In our personal lives and in world affairs our record reads poorly. We have proved inept at handling life; we're not as ready for living as we often like to think we are. But God stands ready to bring order out of our chaos. He loves us and takes the initiative in coming to our rescue.

Unfortunately, we sometimes fail to respond to God, and that constitutes our major problem. When we live mostly on a horizontal plane, we experience little awareness of the vertical dimension of life. We frequently act independently of God, seeking to manage our affairs all by ourselves. Not that we have any conscious quarrel with God. We have simply allowed the temporal affairs of daily life to crowd out the eternal things of the Spirit.

Why?

Our fundamental problem is pride. We want to put our own interests first. Our pride prompts us to act as Jacob did; we seek self-advantage. Pride causes us to put ourselves before God, and herein lies the root of all our sin.

Our pride and self-sufficiency erect brass walls between

us and God, blinding us to our own dilemma and to God's availability. Because we are not in tune with God, we experience disharmony with ourselves and our neighbor. God seems distant, and in our honest moments we worry about it.

We sometimes cover up our spiritual failure by busying ourselves with religious activity. We may, for example, discuss the dynamics of religious structures, but forget the real reasons the structures exist. Though we may bravely wear a facade of religious respectability, on the inside we feel like hollow men.

Instead of calling upon God for help, we try to approach him by human merit. Our pride blinds us to our inability to climb out of the ditch by ourselves. Although we nobly persist in trying to ascend the ladder of human merit, we cannot do so. The Bible makes it eminently clear that natural man has within himself neither the desire nor the ability to find God (for example, see Gen. 6:5; I Kings 8:46; Ps. 53:3; Prov. 20:9; Isa. 53:6, 64:6; Rom. 3:23; Gal. 3:22; I John 1:8, 5:19). But God doesn't wait for us to come to him; he comes to us!

When Adam sinned, he ran from God and tried to hide. One of the most winsome verses in the Bible records God's seeking disobedient man. "Adam, where are you?" sums up God's attitude toward us all.

Egocentricity shapes the religion of man. It is based on human merit, and it caters to pride. By way of contrast, the Christian gospel rests on God's undeserved favor. The gospel consists not in what we do for God, but in what God does for us.

26

God does not sit loftily in heaven, waiting for us to achieve worthiness. He moves toward us in a personal and loving manner, offering us forgiveness and a fresh start. The gospel is not the *bad* news of God's demands and requirements; it is the *good* news of God's gracious offer of life. God is like the father in the parable of the prodigal. God, like that father, lavishes his love and blessing upon his returning son. God's ultimate demonstration of love for us may be seen in the person and ministry of Jesus of Nazareth.

As Christ is the *revelation* of God's love, the Holy Spirit is the *operation* of God's love. The Holy Spirit shows us our need of God. He helps us see our predicament, and he reveals to us Christ, the way out of our spiritual poverty. Naturally, we sometimes resist God's pulling the rug from under our egos. But the Holy Spirit continues faithfully to lead us to see our need of total dependence upon God. Sometimes he even allows us to get into desperate situations so that we become willing to admit our need of him.

Working in our lives, the Holy Spirit leads us to repentance and faith. *Repentance* means turning away from the old; *faith* means turning to the new. Biblical repentance means a complete change of mind, a total change of direction and intention. Biblical faith involves a total trust in Christ, apart from human merit or worthiness.

When, with the help of the Holy Spirit, we place our faith in Christ, we become united to Christ through the miracle of God's grace. The Holy Spirit imparts divine life to us. We become "grafted" into Jesus Christ. As Christians, we enjoy a new relationship with Christ, as close as that of branches to vine; and as a "seal" of God's presence, he sends his Holy Spirit to dwell in our hearts.

Paul asserted, "If any one is in Christ, he is a new creation; the old has passed away, behold, the new has come" (II Cor. 5:17). The new life which Christ gives us is so totally transforming that it can best be described as a new birth. Christian conversion involves a radical reshaping of our personalities. For this reason, coming to know Christ stands out as the most significant experience that can occur in the life of a human being.

Now, let's look at what happens when we personally meet Jesus Christ.

In Christian conversion the Holy Spirit ministers to man's four basic spiritual problems: (1) guilt, (2) estrangement from God, (3) spiritual inadequacy, and (4) lack of purpose and direction. Our new life in Christ results in a new standing, a new relationship, a new spiritual dynamic, and a new call.

The first result of knowing Christ: a new standing. To receive Christ into one's life is to secure a divine pardon. Our guilt is removed, and we experience God's forgiveness as a personal reality. When we accept God's pardon, our "standing" before God is changed. Once we stood condemned; now we stand forgiven.

Guilt has always plagued man as one of his most serious problems. Guilt feelings disable us; they rob us of inner peace, and they blight all we do and think. Man's sense of guilt drags him down, and it hinders creative and joyful living.

When we try to repress guilt, we succeed only in pushing it down into the unconscious mind. Even though it lies buried, it remains dynamic and continues to plague us. Man is unable to stifle successfully the inner monitor of the soul, the conscience. The only adequate solution for guilt is a conscious experience of God's forgiving love.

The Bible refers to forgiveness as *justification* (Acts 13:39; Rom. 3:28, 5:1,18; I Cor. 6:11; Gal. 3:24; Phil. 3:9). Justification means the exact opposite of condemnation. To condemn someone is to hold him guilty; to justify him is to declare him innocent. The Bible uses the term justify to express the idea of God's forgiving man.

Man cannot reconcile himself to God. To seek to do so would be like stealing an automobile and then saying to the owner, "Don't worry about your car; it's all right now because I've forgiven myself." Justification is God's forgiveness of sinful man so that man receives a clean slate. Paul declares, "Therefore, since we are justified by faith, we have peace with God through our Lord Jesus Christ" (Rom. 5:1).

A minister conversed with a man who had taken hard drugs for several years. As they talked, the man related how guilty he felt because his drug habit had wrecked his life and the lives of persons he loved. As he prayed, asking God for pardon and for a new life, God forgave him. Through joyful tears the man said, "I feel clean on the inside for the first time in thirty-nine years."

This man's experience of God's pardon was dramatic. Other persons find God's forgiveness in a quiet way. John Killinger has expressed the following thought: "The coming of the Lord is sometimes like the rushing of a mighty wind, and sometimes the raging of a great fire; but it is also like the sound of silence, or one hand clapping." Whether one reacts dramatically or quietly, the experience of divine forgiveness radically changes one's life.

Until forgiven by God, all persons remain guilty in his sight. One cannot truly be reconciled to God or be freed from his burden of guilt until he receives divine pardon. Experiencing God's forgiveness, we stand justified in his sight, no longer under the condemnation of sin.

The second result of knowing Christ: a new relationship. When we place our faith in Christ, God accepts us as his own children. Paul's epistles refer to this new relationship as *adoption* (Rom. 8:15; Gal. 4:5. See also Deut. 14:2; II Cor. 6:18; Gal. 3:26; Eph. 1:5). Before knowing Christ, we do not enjoy the privilege of true sonship. God is not our Father in a personal sense. But faith in Christ as Savior brings us into membership in God's family. Then we have the privilege of calling God "Father," because he has adopted us as his sons and daughters!

It is only a half-truth to say that God is the Father of us all. When Jesus talked with certain religious leaders who boasted, "We have one Father, even God," Jesus deflated them with these words: "You are of your father the devil" (John 8:41,44). We are all God's *creation,* but we become his *sons* only through personal faith in

Jesus Christ. Scripture invites everyone to become God's child through faith: "He planned, in his purpose of love, that we should be adopted as his own children through Jesus Christ" (Eph. 1:5, Phillips).

When God adopts us into his family we become heirs of Christ's estate. To the new Christians at Rome, Paul wrote, "You have been adopted into the very family circle of God and you can say with a full heart, 'Father, my Father.' The Spirit himself endorses our inward conviction that we really are the children of God." And he adds, "Think what that means. If we are his children we share his treasures" (Rom. 8:15-17, Phillips).

In God's family there exists no separation of race, sex, or position. In the Christian community all Christians belong to one another because each one belongs to God. In fact, only in a truly vital Christian fellowship can the last shreds of prejudice and status be erased.

We do not have to guess about God's attitude toward us. We can have assurance of his acceptance. Christian assurance is a coin with two sides—an objective side and a subjective side.

The objective side of assurance rises out of the definite promises made to us by Christ. For example, he said, "In very truth, anyone who gives heed to what I say and puts his trust in him who sent me has hold of eternal life, and does not come up for judgement, but has already passed from death to life" (John 5:24, NEB). We can have confidence in Christ's word because of who he is. His very character backs up his words. He has said that he receives us as his children when we turn to him in faith; and his word stands solid, utterly reliable.

The inward conviction that God accepts us constitutes the subjective side of assurance. Such confidence is expressed in the gospel song which says, "You ask me how I know he lives—He lives within my heart." Some theologians have given the term "the witness of the Spirit" to this inner conviction that God has accepted us. The apostle John wrote, "By this we know that we abide in him and he in us, because he has given us of his own Spirit" (I John 4:13).

Thus, the certainty of Christ's word and the conviction of inner experience lift the Christian to a confident assurance that he belongs to God. He is no longer estranged from God; he has become God's child. Such certitude frees one to become his true self and to develop under Christ his full potential.

The third result of knowing Christ: a new spiritual dynamic. Christ not only forgives us and receives us into his family—he also imparts to us the power to lead a new life. The Bible calls this *regeneration* (Titus 3:5. See also Ezek. 36:26; John 1:13; II Cor. 5:17; I Peter 1:23; I John 5:1).

The transformation brought about in regeneration is so radical that it may be compared to moving from a geocentric view of the universe to a heliocentric view. One moves from a *self* orientation to a *Christ* orientation.

Spiritual birth stands as a miracle of the highest order. Through the inward working of the Holy Spirit, God imparts to us a new power and inner dynamic. This transformation is nothing less than supernatural. In fact, spiritual regeneration is the *only* adequate cure for the inner sickness of man. When a bishop wrote to John Wesley accusing him of believing in "miraculous conversion," Wesley replied: "Sir, I did not know there was any other kind of conversion except a miraculous one."

While Christian conversion *does* impart new life to every believer, it *does not* produce identical Christians. God created every person as a unique and special human being. God never gives any two Christians exactly the same conversion experience. Although an individual relationship with Christ remains common to all instances of spiritual regeneration, God customizes a personal encounter for each individual. When we try to force every person into the same religious experience, we fail to honor the uniqueness of persons or the creativity of the Holy Spirit.

Common to all conversions, however, is the regeneration of human nature as a result of having received the Holy Spirit. Jesus likened regeneration to a "new birth" because the Holy Spirit replaces spiritual inadequacy with the power of God's life-giving grace.

The fourth result of conversion: a new call. God gives to us a new sense of purpose and direction through the rebirth of the Spirit. Christians are cleansed and called to a life of spiritual growth and service to God. This is called *sanctification* (John 17:17; I Cor. 1:2, 6:11; Eph. 5:26; Heb. 2:11, 13:12; I Peter 1:2; Jude 1). Referring to the new life which the Corinthian Christians had received, Paul wrote, "You were washed, you were sanctified, you were justified in the name of the Lord Jesus

33

Christ and in the Spirit of our God" (I Cor. 6:11). Sanctification means two things: (1) to set apart, to consecrate for service, and (2) to make holy, to cleanse and purify.

"You belong to me, and I have great plans for you." This is the way God feels about every Christian. God sets apart the converted Christian and consecrates him to his service. Since God has an exclusive claim on the Christian and wants to use him in significant ways, he cleanses him in order that he might be a pure vessel and a clean channel.

Sanctification extends to every daily relationship and decision. The Christian finds a new purpose and sense of direction in life because he has been set apart (sanctified) for God's work. Although it takes a lifetime to discover and experience all the implications of sanctification, this process begins with the new birth. Peter wrote a letter to the Christians of his time reminding them that they were "chosen and destined by God the Father and sanctified by the Spirit for obedience to Jesus Christ" (I Peter 1:2). God has a plan for each life—a plan that stretches out into an exciting future. Life is no longer without definite purpose, because in sanctification the Christian finds a reason and a ground for creative living.

Sanctification also denotes *cleansing* or *purifying*. The indwelling of the Holy Spirit results in the reorientation of our affections and the cleansing of our motives. We'll say more about this aspect of sanctification later. At this point, however, it is important to note that sanctification doesn't mean that we are operated on by the Holy Spirit so that sin is removed as a dentist might extract an infected tooth.

Sin isn't a substance or a quantum; it results from a broken relationship between man and God. The Christian is sanctified as long as Christ remains enthroned as supreme Lord in his heart. *Jesus Christ* is "our wisdom, our righteousness and sanctification and redemption" (I Cor. 1:30).

To summarize the results of Christian conversion, Jesus Christ, through the ministry of the Holy Spirit, transforms human life in four ways:

He gives a new standing: the Christian is *justified,* counted as innocent.

He gives a new relationship: the Christian is *adopted,* made a child of God.

He gives a new nature: the Christian is *regenerated,* given a new spiritual life.

He gives a new call: the Christian is *sanctified,* cleansed and commissioned to serve God.

Unfortunately, some well-meaning church people at times tend to minimize the importance of Christian conversion. Some say that social action constitutes the *totality* of the Christian life. Obviously, service to one's fellowman is essential if we are to be obedient followers of Christ. But sweeping statements which *equate* Christian service and Christian faith stress the horizontal dimension of the gospel to the neglect of its vertical dimension. We can find neither the motivation nor the power for service without the working of God's Holy Spirit within our lives.

The church must never lose sight of basics, and the most basic doctrine of the church is that individuals can be changed through a personal encounter with Jesus Christ. Of course, we must involve ourselves in the service of others, but we must do so in the power of the Holy Spirit. Christian conversion remains fundamental to the whole of the Christian life.

There will always be critics who reject the notion that anyone can relate to God in the manner described in this chapter. Usually such skepticism is offered in the name of science or logic; but the work of God in the human heart cannot be limited to the world of human reason, telescopes, microscopes, and blue litmus paper.

Of course it takes faith to believe that God can make you spiritually fit, but it stretches you past the limit to accept the alternative that God can not do so. If you know Christ, you have begun a new existence. God has planted an artesian well of life in your heart; he has sent his Spirit to dwell within. His boundless resources belong to you. Life beckons with all of its fullness—and you are ready to live.

III

Saints Alive

Let us now learn from Holy Scripture
that all believers in Christ are saints.

—Martin Luther

My friend sat on the back steps, shucking corn. He served as my host for several days while I held services at the church he attended. Joining him for a chat, I admired a beautiful potted plant on the porch nearby. He said, "My wife and I were convinced that the plant was dead, so I set it outside to be thrown away. But in the fresh air, sunshine, and rain it grew up from the roots." He went on to observe, "I guess it had life in it all the time."

Christians have life, too. They have received God's grace in their hearts. Christ imparts his life to them through the Holy Spirit, who is called the "Spirit of life" (Rom. 8:2). As Paul expressed it, we become "temples" of the Holy Spirit (I Cor. 3:17, 6:19; II Cor. 6:16). Receiving Christ's life, Christians "become partakers of the divine nature" (II Peter 1:4).

Many Christians seem unaware of the significance of having received the Holy Spirit. Still others appear ignorant even of the fact that their Christian conversion was a "birth" of the Holy Spirit (John 3:5). I once heard a student say, "I was converted three weeks ago, and I received the Holy Spirit yesterday." A postal official reported, "Six people were converted to Christ in our church last Sunday, and two others received the Holy Spirit." A cattle rancher said, "I have trusted Christ as my Lord. Now that I'm a Christian, I'm praying that he will give me his Holy Spirit."

Strictly speaking, such statements do not accord with New Testament teaching. Christian conversion cannot occur apart from a personal reception of the Holy Spirit. Paul insists, "Any one who does not have the Spirit of Christ does not belong to him" (Rom. 8:9).

In receiving the Holy Spirit we do not receive merely *part* of him; God's Spirit can never be divided into portions. The Holy Spirit cannot be partly with you any more than you can be partly in London. Of course, the Christian's knowledge of all the implications of the Spirit's presence will be fragmentary. In fact, an entire lifetime is not long enough for anyone fully to apprehend the depths of the Holy Spirit. But every genuine Christian does have the Holy Spirit.

Jesus in his incarnation was necessarily limited by time and space, but the Holy Spirit is not limited in this way. Although we do not have the physical presence of Christ with us today as the disciples did, through the Holy Spirit he dwells in all true believers everywhere.

Before his ascension to the Father, Jesus said, "I tell you the truth: it is to your advantage that I go away, for if I do not go away, the Counselor [the Holy Spirit] will not come to you; but if I go, I will send him to you" (John 16:7). In actuality, Jesus was saying, "I am going to send the Holy Spirit to take my place. Even as I am with you now, so in the future the Holy Spirit will be with you."

The primary purpose of the Holy Spirit is not to produce spectacular manifestations. Rather, his basic work is to clarify and apply to us the revelation given in Jesus Christ. The Holy Spirit is the Spirit of Christ (II Cor. 3:17). Jesus said, "When the Spirit of truth comes, . . . he will glorify me, for he will take what is mine and declare it to you" (John 16:13,14).

The Holy Spirit communicates Christ's *completed* ministry to us. It was therefore appropriate that the earthly ministry of Christ be finished *before* the Holy Spirit came in his fullness. When Jesus finished what he came to do on earth, he ascended to the Father. Then the fire fell! The Holy Spirit came to usher in the promised day which the prophets had foretold. The day of Pentecost had arrived, bringing in a new era of the Holy Spirit.

The advent of the Holy Spirit at Pentecost will never be repeated in precisely that same way, any more than Christ's resurrection or his ascension will be repeated. Of course, we can participate in the *results* of Pentecost, but Pentecost itself was unique. It introduced a new phase of God's working in the redemption of humanity.

Shortly after the coming of the Holy Spirit at Pentecost, Peter preached an important sermon, explaining what had happened. He based his message on Joel's prophecy. We must remember that Joel lived in a time when the Holy Spirit was given only occasionally to a few persons for the purpose of performing specific tasks. For instance,

Bezalel received the Holy Spirit for skill in his work on the tabernacle (Exod. 35:30-35). The judges received from the Holy Spirit the ability to judge the people (Judg. 3:10). Gideon was anointed for leadership by the Spirit (Judg. 6:34). Samson received the power of the Spirit for physical strength (Judg. 14:6). The Spirit empowered Zerubbabel to rebuild the temple (Zech. 4:6). Daniel was given by the Spirit the gift of wisdom (Dan. 5:11-14). Joel's prophecy, however, pointed to the future, when the Holy Spirit would be poured out in his fullness on all persons!

> And it shall come to pass afterward,
> that I will pour out my spirit on all flesh;
> your sons and your daughters shall prophesy,
> your old men shall dream dreams,
> and your young men shall see visions.
> Even upon the menservants and maidservants
> in those days, I will pour out my spirit (Joel 2:28,29).

Explaining in his sermon what had happened at Pentecost, Peter declared, "This is what was spoken by the prophet Joel" (Acts 2:16-21). In short, the great day had come! Bursting with excitement, the listeners cried out, "What shall we do?"

Peter replied, "Repent [confess your sin] and be baptized [witness publicly to your faith], . . . and you shall receive the gift of the Holy Spirit." That very day, three thousand persons turned to Christ, and they received the Holy Spirit. Since that time, all genuinely Christian conversions are accompanied by the personal reception of the Holy Spirit. (Later in the book we will deal with "being filled with the Holy Spirit.")

In the New Testament, converted Christians are called "saints" because they are "sealed" with the Holy Spirit. For example, Eph. 1:1, 13: "Paul, an apostle of Christ Jesus by the will of God, to the saints who are also faithful in Christ Jesus. . . . In him you also, who have heard the word of truth, the gospel of your salvation, and have believed in him, were sealed with the promised Holy Spirit." Paul's teaching in a nutshell is, "I have good news for you, Christian. You have Christ's life because you have his Spirit. You're a saint; now start acting like it!"

Christians are *saints alive.* In order to become Christlike, Christians are summoned to draw upon the power of the Holy Spirit within them, to rely upon Christ's indwelling presence.

Yet, much muddy thinking abounds regarding the Christian's relationship to the Holy Spirit and what it means to be Christlike. Some hold the view that Christians are only *accounted* righteous. Such reasoning denies any *impartation* of righteousness through the indwelling Holy Spirit. Persons holding this view disavow that the Christian personally receives the presence of the Holy Spirit or that the Christian ever becomes holy. Persons who hold to this point of view believe that God only *looks upon* the believer as righteous rather than actually *making* him righteous. The doctrine of justification by grace alone overshadows all else, and a concern for forgiveness tends to crowd out any belief that Christians can actually be changed within.

Those who hold this view are pointing to an important truth. They seek to give all the glory to God for man's salvation. They want to avoid any semblance of trusting in human worthiness for redemption.

However, it is only a half-truth to emphasize that God merely *reckons* the Christian to be righteous, or that he is concerned exclusively with man's forgiveness. God does more than merely forgive our sin; he also makes us into new persons. Through the Holy Spirit Christians receive the power to lead a transformed life. We might call this inner transformation *realized righteousness*.

At the other end of the spectrum arises a different sort of misunderstanding of the Christian's relationship to Christ. Some persons believe that the Holy Spirit becomes the property of the Christian, and that the Holy Spirit makes the Christian almost independently holy. Christians holding this view speak of holiness almost as a quantum received from God and held as a possession of the Christian. They see the Christian as having been operated on by the Holy Spirit and thereby enabled to perform righteous deeds.

Persons holding this view are pointing to an important truth in trying to take seriously the real change which occurs at Christian conversion. They want to make a place for holy living. But they err in separating holiness from its origin in God. In doing so they tend to de-emphasize the importance of the relational nature of Christian discipleship. As a consequence, moment-by-moment dependence upon Christ is pushed into the background.

Thus, we see two extremes: some Christians believe

that Christ forgives them, but does little to bring about a real change in their nature; still other Christians believe that the Holy Spirit makes them into holy persons, free from any further necessity of repentance.

The truth lies somewhere between these extremes. We can illustrate the nature of the Christian life this way. If you have ever seen a blacksmith at work, you know that when he thrusts a horseshoe into the fire it eventually becomes hot and it glows. The iron horseshoe does not generate its own heat, but as long as it is in the fire, it glows with fire. When removed from the heat, the metal becomes cold.

In a similar manner, Christians who are "in Christ" do not generate or sustain holiness by themselves, but they do partake of *Christ's* holiness. They remain adequate as long as they "abide in Christ." Paul writes that "righteousness [is] imparted to, and operating in, all who have faith in Jesus Christ" (Rom. 3:22, Phillips).

God calls every Christian to be holy: "As he who called you is holy, be holy yourselves in all your conduct" (I Peter 1:15). We mistakenly think that a saint is some rare specimen—someone in a history book, someone mystical or strange. But saints are not persons who walk about in sackcloth. Nor do they necessarily live in monasteries or fast three times a week. In biblical terminology a saint is one who is set apart for the service of God. Saints can be found in factories, in offices, on tractors, or at the kitchen sink. So far as Scripture is concerned, every Christian is a saint, in that each Christian is called to do God's will.

43

When we think of the term saint, we are naturally led to think of another important biblical term—holiness. Unfortunately, the word holiness has suffered many things at the hands of many (theological) doctors. Although the term has been misunderstood and abused, it is a perfectly good word. Holiness is a biblical term, and it is time we rediscovered it. In a number of places in the New Testament, Christians are called to walk in holiness. (Eg. Luke 1:75; II Cor. 7:1; Eph. 4:24; I Thess. 3:13; 4:7; I Tim. 2:15; Heb. 12:10, 14; II Peter 3:11.)

However, several dead-end streets are followed by sincere Christians who are seeking to discover and manifest Christian holiness. These dead-end streets are (1) mysticism, (2) activism, (3) legalism, and (4) religiosity.

First, consider the mystics. Some seek Christian holiness through cultivating inner impressions and religious experiences. They follow subjective impressions or feelings wherever they may lead. Of course, there are certain mystical elements in the Christian life (prayer is, in a sense, mystical); but mysticism which is almost entirely subjective is more harmful than helpful.

I know a three-year-old boy who has a teddy bear named Panda. My little friend tells me that he has conversations with Panda. These conversations and experiences are real to him, but they actually are only the result of his imagination. Adults, too, sometimes get carried away with their impressions. Feelings and inner impressions are quite unreliable as a basis for our religious life.

Feelings can be produced in many ways. They can result from drugs or from not getting enough sleep. One might eat too much of the wrong food for dinner and get a "mystical feeling" clear down in the pit of his stomach! We dare not equate every mystical impression with the Holy Spirit or with the voice of God. Inner impressions often stem from physical or emotional factors, and if we rely solely upon them, we are quite likely to be disappointed.

The contemporary recovery of the ministry of the Holy Spirit should be welcomed. However, if we stress the Holy Spirit to the neglect of Jesus Christ, we run the danger of developing a cult of the Holy Spirit. A student of mine recently told me that in his area of the country a number of churches have replaced the traditional emblem of the cross with the symbol of a dove. As well-intentioned as this shift may be, such a central emphasis on the Holy Spirit fails to grasp the primary function of the Spirit. His basic work is to exalt Jesus Christ, the risen Lord.

When the Holy Spirit is given undue emphasis and our worship centers almost exclusively around him, we can easily permit our inner feelings and experiences to take the place of Scripture as a witness to Jesus Christ. Subjective worship is important, but it must always be based on the objective revelation of God in Christ.

Any thought or action which is not grounded in Scripture is sub-Christian. Christian maturity and Christlikeness never arise from the cauldron of our own subjective feelings. Such impressions may be likened to our looking into a deep well and describing the reflection as "seeing God."

Some within the contemporary drug culture seek religious enlightenment through drugs. One who follows such a route cannot find what he is looking for in this way, nor will the intellectual who trusts almost entirely in his own ideas about God. Even mountaintop experiences do not provide a solid foundation for Christian holiness.

Talking with "spirits" and participating in séances—even in a so-called Christian context—are additional illustrations of unwholesome mysticism. It is not too strong a statement to say that communion with *any* spirit other than the Spirit of the risen Christ is *spiritual adultery*.

In Scripture God strictly forbids praying to, or communing with, anyone but himself. "Christian spiritualism" is not only a contradiction of terms, it is also extremely dangerous. Christ is all that the Christian needs. To seek mystical experiences or to commune with other spirits is to veer off center and risk spiritual confusion.

Christian holiness and Christian maturity come through regular communion with Jesus Christ as he is objectively revealed through the Bible and through the word and sacrament of the church.

Second, there are those who mistake action for holiness. Certainly, some activists would strongly object to the term saint or the word holiness. They would say, "Piety and holiness are irrelevant terms." But in actual fact, activists *are* seeking sainthood, because to be a saint is to do the will of God. Activists seek to do God's will through busyness and social action.

Obviously, Christian faith must be translated into meaningful action or else it ceases to be Christian. But activism becomes man-centered and humanistic if it is cut off from its roots in God.

In Jesus' day the Zealots neglected to cultivate the "inner life." They formed a group of fanatical nationalists who advocated violence as a means of liberating their country from Rome. Their cause dominated all other moral and ethical concerns. Such enthusiasm seems too extreme even to be considered "religious." Nevertheless, causes can grip us to the extent that they become substitutes for deeper spiritual commitments to God.

We must never allow the necessary and desirable social programs of the church to become ends in themselves. To do so would be to reduce the church to another social agency and blind it to man's deeper need of spiritual healing. That we have immature Christians in the church, who do little to translate piety into deeds, is well known. However, activism in itself must not be confused with Christian holiness.

The roots of much of our activism can be traced back to the ancient Greek moralists, who sought to build a closed system of ethics which was completely man-centered, a system totally unrelated to God. For them, "man is the measure of all things." They felt that their actions were self-justifying and needed only the approval of conscience.

But God is infinitely more interested in the reasons and motives behind our activity than he is in the sheer amount of work we attempt. We can immerse ourselves even in religious work and miss Christian maturity altogether.

Recently, a pastor in a midwestern state said to me, "I

have two couples in my church who leave town almost every weekend witnessing for Christ. But they seriously neglect their children, and the people where they work say they are sometimes grouchy and hard to get along with." Activity alone, no matter how zealous, falls short of true Christian holiness.

Balance is, of course, what we need. The spirit of a busy Martha *and* the spirit of a meditative Mary must blend in our lives. In our day, however, we seem to have an overabundance of *doing* at the expense of *being*. Certainly, God desires our service, but he also wants our fellowship. Proper and fruitful activity must flow from adequate time spent in God's presence.

Third, some seek sanctity through slavish obedience to rules. These are the legalists who feel that the stricter the demands, the better the religion. Their motto is "Avoid all appearance of evil." Frequently, legalists embrace rules and regulations which distort biblical teaching. Such action reflects a false holiness rooted in taboos rather than in Jesus Christ.

The best-known illustration of legalism is the sect of the Pharisees which flourished in Jesus' day. Their name derived from the verb *parash,* "to separate." They were the radical puritans of Judaism who withdrew from all evil associations, and who sought to obey an incredibly detailed oral and written code. An example of their legalism may be seen in their refusal to allow on the Sabbath the healing of the sick or the casual plucking of grain for eating. Many Pharisees paraded their good deeds before others in a self-righteous manner. Not all were hypocrites, of course, but many erred in that they were seeking to win God's favor by external obedience to strict rules.

Jesus compared the legalists of his day to a cup scrupulously clean on the outside, but filthy on the inside. They often did laudable deeds, but with the wrong motives. Christ shattered their smugness by showing them that vital religion goes deeper than rules. For this reason they hated him intensely and ultimately crucified him.

Legalism usually develops over a period of time, slowly crystalizing the fruits of love; rules and regulations imperceptibly replace joyful discipline. What once flowed freely as an act of love hardens into a legalistic ordinance. Codified living replaces creative living. When a loving relationship degenerates into a system of dos and don'ts, something is invariably lost in the process.

The legalist commits himself to the law, but not necessarily to Christ. He keeps the letter of the law, but the spirit behind it may escape him. He glories in self-sacrifice, but his religion centers in his own performance rather than in God.

The greatest fault of legalism is that it tends to substitute laws for love. It is committed more to the precepts of Christ than to the person of Christ. Legalism swerves from love into a brittle and inflexible religion—a religion rooted more in duty than in devotion.

Another problem with legalism is that it often adds nonbiblical legislation to the gospel. In doing so, it digs a vast chasm between the church and the world. The gradual accretion of new regulations projects a false impression to others as to the real nature of the gospel. Freedom, spontaneity, and joy cannot flourish where one's basic commitment is given to a system. True Christian holiness develops only as a natural by-product of our relationship to Christ himself.

Fourth, there are those who mistake religiosity for holiness. The religionist trusts in being religiously proper. He places great importance on such things as forms of worship, the sacraments, proper theology, and ecclesiastical traditions. Religionists cannot function without the proper religious trappings.

Christ received his greatest opposition from "religious" people who confined God to their own perception of religion. They were unwilling to admit that God is greater than a system and stands in judgment on all forms of religion. Religion can easily center in man and his moral achievements, but Christianity centers in Jesus Christ.

By all means, a Christian should be loyal to his church. But one's supreme loyalty must be to Jesus Christ, who is Lord of everything, including the church. Someone has said, "At least 50 percent of the history of the church is a liability to its witness." Whether or not that statement is statistically accurate, it does point to the fact that the church is not final.

To be sure, the church is the channel through which God conveys the gospel. And ultimately the church will triumph through God's grace. Nevertheless, at times the church embraces certain human traditions which are not crucial to the gospel and which may even hinder the progress of the gospel. Therefore, the Christian must never give an uncritical commitment to an institutional expression of the Christian faith. His final allegiance is to Christ alone.

Scrupulous adherence to ritual and proper order may get in the way of our participation in the fresh winds of the Holy Spirit. Rabid loyalty to the past can deafen us to any new prophetic word from God. No "wineskin," including orthodoxy, can contain the dynamic and transcendent gospel.

The "traditions of the elders" can become an iron wall between man and God. Religion in itself tends to feed self-righteousness and to hinder the free working of God's Spirit. True holiness and sanctity never come through religion, but only through the indwelling Spirit of Christ. As the Holy Spirit makes Christ increasingly real to us, we grow in his likeness.

Mysticism, activism, legalism, and religiosity—all prove ineffective in producing new life and spiritual maturity.

Christian holiness starts to develop when the Christian begins to celebrate his conversion by allowing Christ's indwelling Spirit to flow unhindered through his thoughts and actions.

Saints who are alive in Christ are not called to achieve adequacy by themselves. They are called to manifest the adequacy of the living Lord. If you are a Christian, you have died to sin, you are buried with Christ, and you have been raised to new spiritual life. Scripture places no limits on your possibilities. You have all of Christ's Spirit! Now the next question is, Does he have all of you?

IV

Falling Off Cloud Nine

If we are clay, let us remember there is a Potter, and His wheel.
—Peter Marshall

Every new Christian feels as if he is on a honeymoon. In a sense, he is. He has discovered in Christ a new joy and inner peace. He feels he is on cloud nine. It is natural for new Christians to feel that they will enjoy their new enthusiasm perpetually.

But sometimes the "honeymoon" loses its radiance. Things fail to go right; spiritual life droops. Then the Christian begins to wonder if his new life is everything he thought it was going to be. He feels discouraged; he becomes disappointed. He asks the question, "What's wrong?"

Probably a couple of things.

First, all of us bring into our Christian lives a certain amount of self-will which we have nourished from birth. And this self-will hinders spiritual growth.

One British university student said, "Six months after my conversion, I discovered there were parts of me that had never yet heard of Jesus Christ." His conversion to

Christ did not stamp out his lifetime habit of putting himself first. Like that student, we all discover times when self-will gets in the way of our doing God's will.

Most Christians sooner or later realize that selfishness has a bulldog grip, and that it is not easy to overcome. Before we can mature as Christians, selfishness has to be seen for what it is: an attitude contrary to God's will. Only when we begin to face our deep-seated self-orientation can significant advances be made in Christian discipleship. A Christian physician prayed, "Lord, I am my own worst enemy. A monster lurks within me. Please take me in hand and deliver me from myself." The man had the courage to acknowledge that apart from Christ's help he was completely inadequate.

Selfishness and egocentricity rise to the surface in many ways: a desire to be first, a reluctance to take criticism, a love of the easy way, a passion always to appear right, a failure to consider the feelings of others.

Even the apostle Paul struggled wtih the problem of self-will. He confessed, "My conscious mind wholeheartedly endorses the Law, yet I observe an entirely different principle at work in my nature. This is in continual conflict with my conscious attitude, and makes me an unwilling prisoner to the law of sin and death. . . . I thank God there *is* a way out through Jesus Christ our Lord" (Rom. 7:21-25, Phillips). Like Paul, contemporary Christians find that they themselves are their own worst hindrance to Christian growth. Pogo, the comic-strip character, gave an excellent commentary on human nature. He once announced, "We have met the enemy, and they is us!"

A second reason Christians sometimes lose the luster from their lives is that they do not fully understand their position in Christ. Jesus taught, "I am the vine, you are the branches. He who abides in me, and I in him, he it is that bears much fruit, for apart from me you can do nothing" (John 15:5). Christians have access to all of Christ's resources, but sometimes in our immaturity we forget that our new life springs from Christ, not ourselves. Christians are branches, not independent vines.

When my youngest son learned to walk, his new achievement produced in him a great degree of over-confidence. He thought that he could climb anything, run anywhere, and leap across any obstacle. His first flush of boldness was boundless. But after several tumbles, he realized that he had limitations.

How much like him most of us are! Changed by God's grace, we tend to believe that we can meet the whole world single-handedly. Our spiritual elation coupled with spiritual inexperience produces overconfidence. We say to ourselves, "Now that I am a new person, I will do great exploits for God." In our enthusiasm we blunder because we trust more in our "religious experience" than we do in Christ.

Most new Christians have too little experience in the Christian walk to know just how powerless they really are in themselves. We just naturally tend to hold an extrava-gant trust in our own ability.

I recently overheard a woman in a retreat ask the song

director to lead in singing her favorite hymn, "How Great Thou Art." She rushed up to him and blurted out, "I wish we could sing that wonderful hymn, 'How Great *I Am.'* " Hers was an honest mistake which any of us might have made. But the phrase, *How great I am,* illustrates how we tend to exaggerate our own ability.

Although Scripture tells us plainly that self-effort is never enough, we Christians sometimes persist in trying to live the Christian life in our own way and in our own strength. A friend related to me that he once drove up to a roadblock which bore a sign, Road Closed. Ignoring the sign, he veered around it and continued down the road. Finally, he came upon two giant road graders blocking any further travel. Attached to one of the machines was a homemade sign. A workman had scrawled, "You fool, I told you so."

Sometimes we ignore the biblical signs that man is mortal and has in himself only limited resources. Certainly man is destined for greatness, but he cannot achieve it apart from divine aid. If we ever get beyond spiritual kindergarten, we must have an understanding of these two things: our limitations and God's unlimited resources.

When our Christian life begins to fray around the edges, nervous tension develops and we become up-tight. Then we begin to experience fear, anxiety and guilt.

Such states of mind constitute too great a load for us to carry. Our bodies and our personalities are not designed to bear the weight of these burdens, so we fall prey to spiritual defeat.

We all tend to live like this at times, don't we? We

seem slow to admit the limitations of our own resources. Writing on this very subject, Paul rebuked the Christians of Galatia by asking them this searching question: "After beginning your experience of God in the Spirit, are you now going to try to complete it by making it dependent upon what human nature can do?" (Gal. 3:3). To depend upon our own natural energy, to neglect to rely upon God, inevitably results in spiritual failures. Christians cannot begin "in the Spirit" and end "in the flesh" if they expect to live victoriously. We Christians are only light bulbs, not power plants.

If these last several paragraphs seem to describe you, then welcome aboard. You're not alone. Since the first century, Christians have had to learn by personal experience their need to rely on the power of the Holy Spirit.

The writer of Hebrews encountered the problem of discouraged Christians. He referred to victorious living as a state of "rest." The sacred writer was certainly inspired when he penned these words: "For anyone who enters God's rest, rests from his own work" (Heb. 4:10). God offers a remedy to Christians who are in a state of tension and anxiety—he has a rest. And Christians experience God's "rest" only as they cease their own striving.

I know a restaurant owner in a southern city, who is a professing Christian; but he has come to the point of nervous collapse. His problem is that he has pushed himself ruthlessly both in his business and in constant endeavor to be an active Christian. Although tense within, he tries hard to be pleasant to his customers so as to be a "good witness." He has for the most part depended entirely upon his own energy, with little reliance upon Christ. He lives as though the entire kingdom of God would collapse without his intense activity. But in the end, he has become physically and spiritually bankrupt. Abundant living has eluded him. He does not function as a free man; he lives as a slave.

To such a person I think Paul would say, "Sir, stop this insanity! You were made for better things. Cease your thrashing about, and turn your striving over to God. He has all the power you need—let Christ live his life through you!"

Although experience ought to be our best teacher, many of us Christians seem slow to learn from our past failures. A shop foreman complained that he was by-passed for a promotion, although he had twenty-five years of experience. But the company president gave this evaluation of him: "He has not had twenty-five years of experience; he has had one year's experience twenty-five times." Similarly, many of us make the same mistakes over and over. We sometimes make tortoiselike progress in learning how to grow in our faith.

Does this mean that Christians are doomed to perpetual frustration and defeat? Not for a minute! The Holy Spirit can provide adequacy for each one of us. Let me illustrate the kind of life that God has provided for every person. Recently, in a Detroit airport, I watched a giant jet plane taxi out to take off for Atlanta. The pilot would not have considered making the entire trip on the wheels of that plane. The huge aircraft was designed to soar, not to inch along a road and become ensnarled in traffic. I watched as the great ship became airborne, disappearing into the vastness of the sky. In a similar manner, God wants his children to be lifted up by the wind of the Spirit to enjoy true freedom.

If you are bothered and uneasy about your spiritual ineptness and failure, your concern is a good sign. A very good sign indeed. Someone said, "The greatest of all faults is to be conscious of none." We do not really "fall from grace" until we cease to care.

What are we to do, then, when we discover that we have no spiritual power in ourselves? What is our recourse in the face of our own egocentricity and our tendency to cater to self-will? What are we to do with our pride, our inadequacies?

There is only one thing to do with your maverick self: *surrender it.* The Christian who has experienced spiritual failure stands in a good position to relinquish his inadequacies to God. He knows by bitter experience how weak he really is. He qualifies better as a candidate for the fullness of the Holy Spirit than one who still lives in the fool's paradise of self-satisfaction. Only those who know themselves to be powerless are in a position to receive God's power. Christ said, "Blessed are those who hunger and thirst for righteousness, for they shall be satisfied."

The price for the fullness of the Holy Spirit is total surrender. But surrender of self is sometimes costly. One of the characters standing trial in *The Brothers Karamazov* is confronted by the prosecutor with these shattering words: "He can be carried off his feet by noble ideals . . . if they need not be paid for." Talking about self-surrender and actually doing it are two different matters. The Spanish have a saying, "He who wants the best must pay the price." It will cost you something to become a maturing Christian. You will have to be willing to pay the price of total dedication to God. But such dedication does not rob us of our humanity, nor is it unpleasant and confining. To "die" with Christ is to be raised by his Spirit into one's true humanity, so that one is liberated to function as God intends.

Most Christians come to new crises of commitment after their conversion to Christ. These new turning points do not arise because God does an imperfect work in us when we are regenerated. Nor do they come because we fail to receive the Holy Spirit at our conversion. From time to time we are faced with the need for deeper commitments, because it takes most of us a period of time to discover how deeply rooted is our desire for self-will. Then, too, only through our failures can we really see how much we need God's power in our lives.

In a young married couples' group, a new bride said, "I knew something was wrong with my Christian life. Things weren't going well at all. Then I realized that my problem was *me. I* was trying to do everything. The Holy Spirit was with me all the time, but I was blocking him by my selfishness." She continued, "Then I turned everying over to Christ, and the Holy Spirit filled me to the brim."

Several of the world religions strive for the annihilation of self or the absorption of self into God. But the destruction of self is neither possible nor desirable. After all, Christ said, "Love your neighbor *as yourself.*"

Self can be integrated around Christ as we are filled with the Holy Spirit. The Holy Spirit doesn't work in Christians to blot them out, but to build them up. Christ did not come to squelch our personalities; he came to redeem and free them.

For most Christians, being "filled with the Holy Spirit" means both a crisis and a process. From time to time, Christians become aware of un-Christlike traits in their lives. As these new insights come, the Christian's normal response should be to invite Christ's Spirit to cleanse and empower his personality at a deeper level. Often these new insights lead to a "crisis" experience of commitment to Christ. Naturally, crises in the Christian life are *beginnings,* not *ends.* And certainly a "crisis experience" does not preclude another crisis later on. In Acts the disciples were "filled with the Holy Spirit" on more than one occasion (Acts 2:4; 4:31; 13:52). The *process* side of being filled with the Holy Spirit involves the ongoing relationship with Christ as Christians "abide" in him.

A frequently asked question is, "How can I be filled with the Holy Spirit?" Perhaps you have raised that very issue. No pat formula can be given because each one of us is a unique individual. However, we all have three things in common: (1) intellect, (2) emotion, and (3) will. Being filled with the Holy Spirit involves our total personality; how we *think,* how we *feel,* and how we *decide.* Let's now look at these three factors.

First, the mind is involved. Our minds are important

because the way we think conditions the rest of our actions. Of course, we never fully understand all the theology of the Holy Spirit, or all the implications of being filled with the Holy Spirit. Nor is it likely that we will ever agree completely on the finer points of doctrine. These are not the crucial issues. The decisive issue is this: Do you believe that God has a larger dimension of living for you through the indwelling presence of the Holy Spirit? Have you apprehended that Christ's promise of abundant life is not a hollow pledge, but a present reality?

If you have doubts, let me offer two suggestions. (1) Study the New Testament. Discover for yourself some of the references which speak of the importance of the ministry of the Holy Spirit. Luke 11:13; 24:49; John 14:16,17,26; 16:12-14; Rom. 8:1-27; I Cor. 2:9-13; II Cor. 3:2-8, 15,16; and Gal. 5:16-25 are but a few such passages. (See also my book *Dynamic Discipleship,* Fleming H. Revell Co., 1973, pp. 87-102.) As you open yourself to the teachings of Scripture, you discover that you can become an adequate person *only* through the fullness of Christ's Spirit. Spirit-filled living constitutes God's norm for all Christians. (2) Tarry before God in prayer. Expose yourself to the searching of the Holy Spirit. Wait in God's presence; ask him to point out your spiritual needs. Such searching demands a radical kind of honesty, but truthfulness with God yields a great harvest.

You may not express yourself eloquently. You may be lacking in a perfect theology. God is impressed, however, with a Christian whose attitude is one of radical self-surrender. A minister told me of an unlettered sheet metalworker in his congregation. This man was a Christian, but he was not living abundantly. He prayed, "O Lord, you know how powerless I am. I just can't seem to do right, and I really need your help. So, Lord, will you please galvanize me?" God answered that prayer because the man confessed his spiritual need, and because he trusted God to give him a needed power.

To open your mind to God and to realize that the fullness of the Holy Spirit is God's will for you is an enormous step in the right direction.

Second, the emotions are involved. Again, honesty is crucial. When we ask God for his help, we do so because we deeply *feel* our need. Many of us can witness to times when personal spiritual failure compelled us to turn to God for his aid. As long as we are content with our own efforts and our present level of Christian maturity, we are not likely to ask God for a greater fullness of his Spirit.

Western man tends to fear emotion, especially in religion. Many of us have been greatly influenced by eighteenth-century enlightenment thought. The rationalism that developed in that century was a legitimate protest against emotional attachments to ideas and institutions. What had happened was this: medieval man embraced religion without thinking very deeply about the *reason* behind his commitment. One critic of a certain group of Christians mocked that they wore hats everywhere they went in order to conceal the cracks in their heads!

Thus, the Enlightenment was born out of a protest against shallow commitments and ungrounded prejudices. The Enlightenment appealed to "sweet reason," and it caused people to think about their presuppositions. Emphasizing the cool head, the Enlightenment looked with disdain on all sorts of "enthusiasm" (emotionalism).

The Enlightenment had its good points. It stimulated science, it encouraged peace between nations, and it helped stem the tide of religious persecution. But with all its good, the Enlightenment was not an unmixed blessing.

Rationalism overreacted against feeling and emotion in religion. In seeking to jettison all forms of emotional excesses, the Enlightenment did us a disservice in insisting that emotion had no place at all in religion.

Particularly in Germany, Great Britain, and the United States, we have continued to follow this line of thinking; and our trust in reason has tended to freeze our emotional lives. All this has resulted in modern man being semi-starved for a personal and satisfying religious experience. In fact, the lack of emotional elements in religion has spawned interesting contemporary reactions as the drug culture, the revival of Eastern religions, and the emphasis upon external manifestations of the Spirit in the so-called Charismatic movement.

What it all boils down to is this: man is, among other things, an emotional being, and feelings must be allowed their rightful place in religious experience. Religion must go further than merely intellectual conviction. It must also reach down to where we *feel*. The growing Christian doesn't hesitate to acknowledge his inward sense of a personal dependence upon God. He does not stifle his emotions—he asks God to use them to help him draw closer to Christ.

Third, the will is involved. To be filled with the Holy Spirit, the Christian must exercise his will in total self-surrender to Christ. Paul stresses the importance of the will: "Do not yield your members to sin as instruments of wickedness, but yield yourselves to God as men who have been brought from death to life" (Rom. 6:13). Paul is writing to Christians about *a definite act of the will.*

The part of your personality that no one else can control is your freedom of choice. God himself will not violate the integrity of your personality. Our wills remain as the last and final barrier between us and the fullness of God's Spirit; and, at the same time, our wills can open the door for the Holy Spirit's gracious working. Our freedom of will is grounded in the "image of God" in man. Nothing can alter the fact that we have the power to say no to God.

In order to be filled with the Holy Spirit you must come to God in the spirit of this prayer: "Not my will, but your will be done." Of course, that is not an easy prayer! But it will bring results if prayed from the depths of the heart. As we confess, God forgives. As we yield, God cleanses. As we consecrate, God fills.

If you have fallen off cloud nine, God offers you a new filling of his Spirit. The flapping of the wings of human endeavor is no substitute for resting upon the "wind" of the Holy Spirit. You need not taxi hopelessly along the ground. You will receive power when the Holy Spirit comes to you in a new fullness. You can mount up on the wings of the Spirit. And then you will soar!

V

Becoming What You Are

Happiness is neither within us only, or without us;
it is the union of ourselves with God.

—Blaise Pascal

One fall I transplanted a maple tree from the nursery into our front yard. I waited through a long winter to find out what my tree would do. Would it grow or wouldn't it? When spring came, it began to put on new green leaves, making remarkable progress.

Like that maple tree, Christians have been transferred out of their old life. They have been transplanted into the kingdom of God. Some have experienced a long winter of dormancy. It is now time for them to begin sending out adventurous roots of faith into the limitless resources of God.

One of the most needful things in the contemporary church is for us, Christians, to face the chasm between our performance and our potential. We all have an "achievement gap" to overcome. God intends, through the ministry of the Holy Spirit, that Christians "should be shaped to the likeness of his Son" (Rom. 8:29, NEB). In Christ, we Christians are called to "become what we are."

Once, while sitting in a restaurant, I noticed an elderly couple at the next table. The husband took a sip of his iced tea and remarked to his wife, "This tea needs more sugar."

She took one glance and replied, "Herbert, you already have a lot of sugar in the bottom of your glass. Stir up what you've got."

Paul told the youthful pastor, Timothy, "Stir up the gift of God, which is in thee" (II Tim. 1:6, KJV). Only by allowing Christ to unleash our potential through his indwelling Spirit can we as Christians become what we are.

The Christian life can be compared to a school. But it is not a university with large classes and computerized answers to be memorized. It compares better to a Master–disciple relationship, with private tutoring by the Holy Spirit, leading each disciple at his own best pace. The Spirit uses three avenues in helping us to mature: (1) Scripture, (2) the church, and (3) personal experiences.

First, the Holy Spirit uses Scripture. The Bible is a unique book and the Christian's source for religious truth. The same Holy Spirit who inspired the biblical writers will also minister to us as we read Scripture today.

It is interesting to compare the Christian Bible to the Koran. For the Muslims, Allah has revealed himself literally in the *words* of the Koran. They feel obligated to go to such extremes as washing their hands in the exact manner prescribed in the Koran. They take its words *literally,* as coming verbatim from Allah. Scripture is, for the Muslims, the "word become word."

Christians, however, believe that God has revealed

himself in Jesus Christ, "Word become flesh." In Christ we see God, and in the Bible we have an inspired and authoritative record of Christ's ministry and message. Christians do not view the Bible in the same light as the Muslims view the Koran. The church regards the Bible as communicating God's truth in language that sometimes must be seen as illustrative. For instance, Jesus said, "If any one comes to me and does not hate his own father and mother and wife and children and brothers and sisters, yes, and even his own life, he cannot be my disciple" (Luke 14:26). Christians interpret this saying as having a *relative* meaning, not a *literal* meaning.

The Bible is not meant to be a rule book for us, containing specific answers for all possible questions. If it were, its size would be completely impractical. Moreover, the Bible would need regular additions as new generations produced new problems. The Scriptures compare more to a father's letters to his children than they do to a cookbook or a how-to-do-it manual.

The Bible serves two important functions for the Christian.

One function has to do with the Bible as *a witness to Jesus Christ*. The ultimate revelation of God is Jesus Christ, but without the Bible our knowledge of Christ would be limited to unreliable oral tradition. The pages of the Old Testament present a record of God's mighty acts in history, preparing the world for the incarnation of Christ. The New Testament tells about Christ's ministry and teaching (the Gospels) and reflects on its results and implications (the Epistles). The authors of the books of the Bible wrote in order that we might encounter God. Therefore, in coming to the pages of Scripture, we should first of all seek him.

As an additional function, the Bible furnishes principles *for guidance in Christian living.* As an illustration, the Bible doesn't directly say whether or not squandering our natural resources or smoking tobacco is sinful. But the Bible does contain a number of principles, all of which are relevant and applicable to daily life.

The Christian who wants to develop his full potential in Christ wants to know the biblical principles. For this reason he studies the Bible with interest. He finds that as he lives in harmony with Scripture, Christ frees him to experience fullness of joy and creativity. With the psalmist of many centuries ago, the Christian says that "his delight is in the law of the Lord, and on his law he meditates day and night" (Ps. 1:2). *Law* here is closely synonymous with the "Word of God"; it is not restricted to specific commands, as for example, the Ten Commandments.

Thus, in the Bible we are pointed to the living Word, Jesus Christ, and to the precepts of God which set us free to become whole persons.

Each new generation needs to be exposed to the Bible as God's corrective for human traditions, faulty notions, and unwarranted prejudices. A Michigan pastor told me that he once served a congregation that desperately needed to renovate its sanctuary. For years, however, the congregation had been fearful of remodeling because a tall column stood in the center of the sanctuary. The members of the church thought that the column supported the roof and to remove it would be dangerous. So the pastor secured a long ladder and took a look. To his surprise he discovered that there was a three-inch gap between the top of the column and the roof! The high pillar supported nothing but the fear of the congregation.

Often the Bible serves as a ladder to allow us to get a proper perspective. As we read Scripture, we are led to see things from God's side. Since we are frequently bound by human tradition, Paul prayed the following: "We are asking God that you may see things, as it were, from his point of view by being given spiritual insight and understanding" (Col. 1:9, Phillips). Certainly, the Bible is our best source for spiritual illumination.

Karl Barth once said, "I discovered a strange new world in the Bible." We all find his affirmation to be true for us as we begin to digest the contents of Scripture. The Bible remains indispensable for the Christian on his way to maturity.

Second, we are helped by the church. God often speaks to us through other Christians. Sometimes, however, we are not very good listeners. I met a new Christian convert at a large midwestern university who said to me, "All the churches are irrelevant. I don't believe in churches. I just believe in doing my own thing for Jesus."

This person made a serious mistake; he cut himself off from over nineteen hundred years of Christian history. His self-imposed exile from the Christian community could only result in his stunted spiritual growth and limited maturity. No one claims that the organized church contains all wheat and no tares. We can always find Christians who poorly represent Christ and his gospel. But the church does belong to Christ, and it provides a regulative setting to aid us in keeping our balance. The church contains the collected wisdom and experience of the centuries. And in the church we find fellowship with other dedicated Christians who can help us mature in our Christian experience.

A mistake sometimes made by renewed persons and movements is to think that they have received all the truth, and that others have little or no truth at all. Sometimes such persons tend to judge others as "not spiritual." Renewal movements often call attention to a much-needed truth, but they also run the danger of emphasizing their particular truth out of proportion, while neglecting other truths needed for perspective. The result usually distorts the Gospel and opens the possibility of fanaticism. All Christians profit from fellowship with the church. Each Christian needs to maintain communication with other Christians, even when he does not perfectly agree with them.

The church, in turn, exercises wisdom when it acknowledges the value of renewed persons within its ranks. Even though newly converted Christians may act in immature ways at times, the church needs to affirm their zeal and sincerity. Present-day church leaders face the responsibility of nurturing new converts in the ways of Christ. Church leaders must avoid any reactionary rejection of persons in their charge, even though such persons may sometimes act rashly or overzealously.

Some of the most tragic chapters in the history of the church have been written because the established church refused to recognize the movements of renewal in her midst. And, at the same time, renewed Christians have sometimes spurned fellowship with the organized church and have sown the seeds of discord and division. Someone has well said, "None of us is as smart as all of us." For balance, all Christians need all Christians.

Every Christian belongs to the church, which is the body of Christ, and belonging to Christ, he also belongs to every other Christian as a joint member in the body. To the church alone, Christ has given the commission to administer the word of God and the sacraments, both of which aid in the full development of the Christian.

The fellowship in Christ's church is superior to any other fellowship. In fact, the bonds between Christians are often more meaningful than those between members of the same family. God never intended for any Christian to function as an isolated unit. As we open ourselves to other Christians in fellowship and love, we grow. As imperfect as it may be, the church belongs to Christ, and he promised to sustain it. The Christian community, along with the Bible, stands as another "means of grace" for the maturing Christian.

Third, personal experiences are important avenues through which Christ works in our lives. The German theologians have a saying: "You have to know a person as your wife before you really know her as your wife." When I first heard that statement, I regarded it as somewhat trite. But as I thought about the saying, I realized that experience reveals more about marriage than books or discussions ever could.

You can learn to ride a bicycle only by riding a bicycle. You can be a Christian only by being a Christian. Even your experiences of failure can contribute to growth; each defeat can become a source of learning. Even in the midst of spiritual frustration, one can see the profound depths of Christ's love. Through the wisdom of experience we discover how much we really need the power of the Holy Spirit in all that we do.

Most of us want to find an immediate panacea which will solve all future problems. We seem to have an itch for the instantaneous. We wish for a spiritual "capsule" to swallow so as to be relieved of further conflict. Sometimes people seek religious experiences which have no basis in Scripture. For example, one man said that he was asking God to make him perfect so that he would never be tempted again. Such idealism is neither realistic nor biblical.

When the Holy Spirit comes into a person's life, he cleanses *attitudes*. As we have noted, sin is not a thing or a substance which can be dealt with as a gardener might deal with a weed. Sin results from wrong attitudes and wrong relationships. Paul writes "The carnal attitude is inevitably opposed to the purpose of God" (Rom. 8:7, Phillips). Paul is saying that carnality is a distortion of our attitudes resulting in broken fellowship with God. Our carnal attitudes, which resist God's purposes for our lives, can be cleansed and brought into submission to Christ.

Such deliverance was the subject of much of Paul's writing in the New Testament.

Let's illustrate God's cleansing of our carnal attitudes this way. Suppose a light is turned on in a dark room. As long as the light burns, no darkness exists. But as soon as the light is turned out, the darkness returns. The darkness is not destroyed; it is *replaced* by light. As long as the Christian is yielded to Christ, carnal attitudes are dispelled by the Holy Spirit.

Once a student named Jim said to me, "I want God to 'zap' me so I can be holy once for all." I asked him if he were a Christian. He said he was, but that he wanted all hindrance to his Christian life eradicated. I pointed out that *anything* can become a hindrance to the Christian life—sex desire, hunger for the approval of others, the drive to achieve. God never extinguishes these drives, because they are not evil in themselves. They can be used for evil purposes (in which case they become carnal), or they can be cleansed by the Holy Spirit and dedicated to Christ.

It is not God's purpose to "zap" us so that we become autonomously righteous; but he will cleanse our faulty attitudes by the power of the Holy Spirit, and through the Spirit's working we can be made victorious over willful sin.

I talked with a man in a northern state who had committed adultery only six days after his commitment to Jesus Christ. Ray was amazed that he should fall into such a sin. He told me that he thought when he was converted to Christ, the sin of lust would be annihilated.

He didn't think he was any longer capable of adultery because Christ had come into his life.

I told him that as long as he was trusting in Christ he *was* cleansed from this sin, and that in Christ he had the power to resist further temptation. Ray had trusted in his religious experience to keep him pure. When he got out of touch with Christ, he fell back into yielding to his former weakness.

The important question for the Christian is not, Have you received the Holy Spirit? The crucial question is, Does Christ have all of you? If you have committed your life to Christ, you have his Spirit. The relevant issue is, Are you continuing to yield your total self to God, and are you constantly open to the fullness of the Spirit's operation in your life?

In the New Testament the Greek verbs for our relationship with God regularly appear in the present tense. The verbs "trust," "filled," and "abide" serve as good examples. They are properly translated, "continue trusting," "keep on being filled," and "perpetually abide." When Paul wrote, "Be filled with the Spirit" (Eph. 5:18), he literally meant, "Keep on being filled with the Spirit."

Naturally, becoming a mature Christian means that obstacles must be faced. If Christian maturity came with perfect ease, most Christians would be mature. "Becoming what you are" must necessarily take place in the context of conflict and opposition. In the New Testament, the Christian life is sometimes even compared to warfare: "For the desires of the flesh are against the Spirit, and the desires of the Spirit are against the flesh; for these are opposed to each other" (Gal. 5:17). Some additional scriptures that refer to the Christian life as warfare are Rom. 7:23; II Cor. 10:4; Eph. 6:12; I Tim. 1:18, 6:12; II Tim. 2:4.

Christians have to contend with their own physical and emotional states while at the same time contending with the pressures of others who are not committed to Christian discipleship. Moreover, demonic forces are rampant in our culture. Our grandparents were right when they spoke of the "temptations of the world, the flesh, and the devil."

The beauty of the Christian way, however, is that conflicts can become opportunities for growth. The Christian can rise above opposition as the eagle rises above air currents. Even our greatest hurdles can teach us to rely more completely on Jesus Christ.

Christian discipleship may be compared to a marriage. You do not have to decide each new day whether you will be married. This should be a settled issue; and you need not be equivocal about your marriage commitment. As a Christian, you do not have to decide each day whether you belong to Christ. You can settle that issue permanently, and you can reach a point of stability in your commitment to Christ which can lift you above vacillation.

The Christian life is never automatic. At conversion, Christ doesn't shove something like a cassette tape into our lives to operate mechanically. He does, however, bring us into union with himself. He promises to be with us always, making available to us the resources of God. Since our Christian life is not automatic, Jude exhorts, "Keep yourselves in the love of God" (Jude 21).

The Christian life consists largely of discipline in the small and seemingly minor daily decisions. Much of life is made up of the little things. A number of years ago a man walked from San Francisco to New York City. His greatest problem during this walk was not the mountain ranges, the rivers, or even the speeding automobiles. His most formidable challenge was the annoyance of small grains of sand which got into his shoes. One of our biggest problems is to learn how to live above the small obstacles of daily life. Vital people, who live above their circumstances, have learned to rely upon the power of the Holy Spirit in little things as well as big things.

There are times when the Christian follows Christ even though he does not feel much like it. He walks by faith. It is astonishing, though, how the awareness of God's presence breaks through to us in the midst of a "dark night of the soul." John stated, "The victory that defeats the world is our faith" (I John 5:4, NEB). Maturing Christians do what they *know* to be right, not what they *feel* to be right.

Now let's turn to the subject of sanctification. If we are to become mature Christians, we need to come to grips with what the Bible teaches about this important subject.

A summation of the New Testament teaching on sanctification might go something like this: all Christians are sanctified in *position,* but not all are sanctified in *practice.* The New Testament teaches that Christ sanctifies us, and it also teaches that we are to sanctify ourselves. Is this a contradiction? Not really. Let me explain.

When I was a boy, I joined the scouts. I got my tenderfoot badge and I became a full-fledged member of the troop. But other concerns crowded in, and I temporarily lost interest. I seldom attended the scout meetings and I made little progress in scouting. One day the scoutmaster confronted me: "Young man, you are a member of the Boy Scouts of America. Why not start becoming a real scout?"

The scoutmaster's challenge was just what I needed. I jumped into scouting with all I had. Making steady progress, I became a scout in actual practice. As a scout, I started becoming what I was.

Paul threw out a similar challenge to the Roman Christians: "Let us never forget that our old selves died with him [Christ] on the cross that the tyranny of sin over us might be broken. . . . Look upon yourselves as dead to the appeal and power of sin but alive and sensitive to the call of God through Jesus Christ our Lord. Do not, then, allow sin to establish any power over your mortal bodies in making you give way to your lusts" (Rom. 6:6, 11-12, Phillips).

The apostle never ordered Christian converts to die to sin; he told them they had *already* died to sin (Rom. 6:2, 11; Gal. 5:24; Col. 3:3). And having died to sin, they were to deal a mortal blow to their *sinful actions*. In other words they were to quit sinning! They were to act like the saints they were in Christ. Paul wrote to the Corinthians, "Come to your right mind, and sin no more" (I Cor. 15:34).

Because of the *position* of these early Christians, Paul urged them on to a fitting *practice*. "I implore you by

God's mercy," he wrote, "to offer your very selves to him: a living sacrifice, dedicated and fit for his acceptance, the worship offered by mind and heart. Adapt yourselves no longer to the pattern of this present world, but let your minds be remade and your whole nature thus transformed" (Rom. 12:1-2, NEB). Sanctification is nothing more or less than becoming all Christ wants us to be.

More than any other thing, Christians need to dedicate themselves fully to Jesus Christ and to deal ruthlessly with any tendency to disobey him. The following verse is representative of Paul's message to Christian believers: "I entreat you . . . as God has called you, live up to your calling" (Eph. 4:1, NEB).

Because Christ's Spirit dwells within, Christians are new people. Christ is their new environment. Each of us is called to respond to the Holy Spirit so that our full humanity may be sanctified.

VI

Hearing From God

Prayer at its highest is a two-way conversation—
and for me the most important part is listening to God's replies.
—Frank C. Laubach

During the last few days before his crucifixion, Jesus told the disciples a good deal about the Holy Spirit. What he said cuts across much of our normal way of thinking about God's working. Although Jesus said much about the Holy Spirit, we have not been as attentive as we should.

One of our problems is that we spend more time talking about God than listening to God. We like to put spiritual concepts into neat filing drawers within our minds. We feel most comfortable when we are in control of religious matters, including God. We sometimes even develop ideas that fail to harmonize with the Bible. When we follow this pattern, we act as if what we say is as important as what God says.

Again and again, we need to be reminded that we are finite and that God is infinite. When it comes to religious truth, we need a guide. Revelation about God doesn't begin with our thoughts; it begins with God's self-disclosure. Christian revelation doesn't consist of man's brilliant insights about God; Christian revelation consists of what God says to man. More than anything else, man needs to hear from God.

God has spoken most definitively to us in Jesus Christ. And, as we have seen, the Holy Spirit is God's primary agent in revealing Christ to us. The Holy Spirit does much more than lead us into knowledge about God. He also works within us so that head knowledge becomes a reality in the heart. He leads us from ignorance to understanding and experience. The Holy Spirit vitalizes religion because he is God in the present tense, actively at work in our lives.

Perhaps the best statement on the work of the Holy Spirit in this regard is the one given by Jesus himself in John 16:7-15. These verses constitute a digest of what Jesus taught the disciples about the Holy Spirit during his final hours with them. He said that his Spirit would come to dwell with the disciples. And then he spoke of three areas of the Spirit's working:

(1) The Holy Spirit convinces men of sin, of righteousness, and of judgment.

(2) The Holy Spirit guides men into all truth.

(3) The Holy Spirit glorifies Christ.

These three aspects of the work of the Holy Spirit represent a summary of his present ministry and tell us how men will hear from God.

First, the Holy Spirit convinces men of sin and of righteousness and of judgment (John 16:8). We realize our sin and become aware of our spiritual needs only through the work of the Holy Spirit.

The Jewish leaders who felt justified in demanding Jesus' crucifixion were convinced in their own minds that they were doing a service for God. Whatever may have been their convictions, they were not convinced that they had any sin. Later, however, some of these same leaders, listening to a sermon by Peter, were cut to the heart with the realization of what they had done. They cried, "Brethren, what shall we do?" (Acts 2:37). Their complete reversal of attitude resulted from the Holy Spirit working in their lives.

Often Christians report that the Holy Spirit has shown them sin of which they were unaware. A Christian lumberman said, "For years I had considered myself a good Christian. Then one day I heard a black person give a speech. As he was speaking, the Holy Spirit showed me some deep resentments toward nonwhites that I had in my heart." On another ocasion a minister confessed, "The Spirit helped me to realize that I was working hard to prepare good sermons in order to receive the praise of my congregation."

None of us is free from the need of having the Holy Spirit point out our weaknesses and our sins. The best Christians need this ministry of God's Spirit. There is a good reason for the Spirit's not showing us all our spiritual needs at one time. Such an experience would indeed be devastating, producing only paralyzing frustrations. We could scarcely cope with such a complete disclosure of our true selves.

So for most of us, understanding our spiritual needs is a continuing process. As fast as we are able and willing to receive knowledge about ourselves, the Spirit ministers to us, revealing new areas of need. The better we know Christ, the more we see our unworthiness. The spiritually mature apostle, St. Paul, called himself "the chief of sinners." He had walked with Christ for decades and had come to a deep understanding of himself. As we respond to the Holy Spirit, he faithfully shows us our sins and our weaknesses.

The Spirit reveals sin in our lives in order to prepare us to receive Christ's forgiveness and healing. The Spirit of Christ continues Christ's ministry, which was not to condemn the world, but to save it.

What did Jesus mean when he said that the Holy Spirit also convinces us of righteousness? New Testament students do not all agree. But a probable meaning is that the Holy Spirit shows us *Christ's* righteousness and worthiness. As the Spirit discloses our need to us he also reveals Christ's love.

We need to see Christ as truly God. People call him a good man, a noble example, and a great religious leader. These qualities seem evident. Christ, however, is much more than the best of men. He is God's own Son—the divine Lord. The Holy Spirit awakens us from preoccupation with ourselves, and refocuses our attention on Christ.

On the cross, Christ was scoffed at by two thieves. But in a short space of time, one of the thieves changed from cursing Christ to worshiping him. To his fellow criminal he said, "This man has done nothing wrong." The Holy

Spirit had convinced him of Christ's righteousness so that he reversed his whole attitude toward him. The Spirit did the same for the centurion at the foot of the cross and for Paul during the three days following his experience on the Damascus road.

Contemporary man needs desperately to see that Christ is not one option among many. Christ is the *only* option which leads to life. While God uses the testimony of others to point to Christ, ultimately it is the Holy Spirit who convinces us that Christ alone is worthy of total devotion. Paul said, "Not having a righteousness of my own, based on law, but that which is through faith in Christ" (Phil. 3:9).

The Holy Spirit also convinces us of judgment. He brings to us the certainty of meeting God in a future accounting. Through the Spirit, we are sobered, made to think, forced to face the future.

A very wealthy lady from New Mexico told of her conversion to Christ: "I had everything," she said. "There wasn't anything I couldn't buy. I had several cars, a lavish wardrobe, three homes, and all the luxuries I wanted. Slowly, I began to realize that something was missing. I wasn't sure what it was, but I knew I wasn't really happy."

Then she said, "I thought to myself that there is probably more to life than just living, and there is probably more to death than just dying. I began to apprehend that I was going to meet God someday in judgment. And that thought changed my life." The Holy Spirit had cut right through all her materialism and convinced her of a coming judgment.

A prominent theological professor related the following story. "A few years after my conversion to Christ, I gradually began to coast along in my Christian life. That is, I became lazy, and I was accomplishing very little. The less I acomplished, the more unhappy I became. I was becoming like the man in one of Jesus' parables who was hiding his talent in the earth."

"One day," he continued, "while reading in Galatians, this verse leaped out at me: 'Do not be deceived; God is not mocked, for whatever a man sows, that he will also reap.' The Holy Spirit helped me to see that some day my life would be judged, and that I couldn't reap where I had not sowed.

"Then," he said, "as God's Spirit helped me to face myself, I surrendered my lethargy to Christ and asked him to forgive me. I prayed that God would fill me with a new energy and anoint me with a new vision. He answered my prayer. With his help I began to tackle projects I had been putting off. I found myself actually enjoying the work I had been avoiding."

Like that professor, all Christians from time to time need the ministry of the Holy Spirit to reveal God's judgment in certain areas of their lives. When we receive this faithful ministry, our best course of action, naturally, is to thank God and repent. Someone has said that repentance begins when we agree with what God says about us.

Seeing our needs is a normal part of Christian growth. We need not be ashamed of having needs. Our only shame is to refuse to acknowledge them.

Second, the Holy Spirit will guide men into all truth (John 16:13). Truth tunnels out before us like an unexploited diamond mine, inviting us to take what we will. We have appropriated but a fraction of what can be ours. It is the task of the Holy Spirit to lead us into greater and still greater discoveries of truth, dim to us at first, but brilliantly illuminating later.

Jesus told his disciples, "There is so much more I want to tell you, but you can't understand it now. When the Holy Spirit, who is truth, comes, he shall guide you into all truth. (John 16:12,13, TLB). Jesus wanted to share many things with his disciples, but they were not yet mature enough to understand them. God is now revealing those things to us through his Spirit.

The Holy Spirit is a master teacher who unfolds truth to us in a patient way. He understands that we can be led only as we are able to comprehend, so he meets us where we are and ministers to us there.

Jesus Christ remains God's supreme revelation to the human family. Jesus, however, is more than a person talked about in the New Testament. He arose from the dead, and now he is actively involved in history. Through his Spirit he continues to reveal truth to mankind.

Christ's Spirit is never static; he is always active. Day by day and year by year, he guides the Christian into a greater understanding of God's ways. And century by century, the Spirit beckons the church to a larger grasp of truth.

No denomination, no catechism, no theologian has ever fully apprehended all the implications and applications of Jesus Christ as God's revelation. We understand only in part. For this reason the Spirit perpetually shows new truth to the church.

We have great theologians of the church: Augustine, Aquinas, Luther, Calvin, Wesley, Barth, and many others. From each one we should gratefully learn. None of these men, however, had a complete understanding of truth. While many of the former insights of the church remain valid, we must go beyond them today.

For example, none of the church fathers was faced, as we are, with such issues as ecology, depth psychology, or the population explosion. God has fresh new truth for us on issues of our day—provided we are open to his Spirit. If they were to come among us today, the great theologians of the past would doubtless want to revise their books in the light of the new truths understood in our time.

Jesus promised that the Holy Spirit would lead us into *all* truth. This phrasing suggests that God's Spirit reveals more than religious truth. Truth is truth, regardless of its area of application. God is interested in the whole of our existence: spiritual, emotional, intellectual, and physical. New discoveries in medicine, science, and agriculture are also gifts of God. The revelation of every new truth results from the operation of God's Spirit.

We need not confine the Spirit's illumination to religious truth. Such a restriction severely limits his ministry. God is interested in the whole world. We must not forget that God so loved *the world* that he gave his only Son. Paul reminds us that "the creation itself will be set free from its bondage to decay and obtain the glorious liberty of the children of God" (Rom. 8:21). Yes, God is interested in all things—every minute detail of his vast universe. In fact, his first covenant was not with Israel, but with Noah and the entire creation. The last promise in the Bible concerns not only the church; it is the promise of a new heaven and a new earth! The Holy Spirit wants to enter into every concern of humanity and lead men into the truth which liberates them and makes them whole.

Thus, *all* Christians need the ministry of the Holy Spirit in finding truth. For this reason prayer ought to be as much a part of the life of a lay person as it is of a Christian minister. The Holy Spirit works in any area which we open to him.

People sometimes say, "I know that God speaks to us through the Bible, but does he ever speak *directly* to us?" At the risk of being misunderstood, I believe he does. Let me explain what I mean.

Our quiet time with God ought to consist of more than praying and reading the Bible. Throughout Christian history and in our own time, many persons tell of the values of *meditating* and *listening*. As we wait receptively in God's presence, he will "speak" to us. Not that he utters audible sounds, but he does make himself known.

As we "listen," his Spirit gives us insight into such matters as:

—Jesus Christ

—ourselves

—the Bible

—some course of action
—the nature of our discipleship in the world.
Sometimes God affirms us; sometimes he rebukes us; sometimes he enlightens us.

The point I'm making is that we can hear from God if we listen for him to speak. It is certainly safe to say that none of us has fully taken advantage of the promise found in Jeremiah (33:3): "Call to me and I will answer you, and will tell you great and hidden things which you have not known."

I believe that there are shades of truth that you as an individual can apprehend better than anyone else. You possess a unique personality, an unmatched set of experiences, a special responsibility, a one-of-a-kind mind. God wants to reveal truth to you as well as to the theologians, the scientists, and the scholars. You have your own unequaled "receiving equipment," and you have a special contribution to make as you allow the Holy Spirit to guide you into truth.

Third, Jesus said of the Holy Spirit: "He will glorify me, for he will take what is mine and declare it to you" (John 16:14). One of the main emphases of this book has been to show that the supreme task of the Holy Spirit is to glorify Jesus Christ and to make him known to us. Some Christians fail to see this. They seem only to want the Holy Spirit to give them an emotional or religious "kick."

One lady said, "I want the Holy Spirit in my life so I can feel all bubbly inside." A college student said, "I'm praying that the Holy Spirit will give me a spiritual 'trip.' " A businessman said, "I am interested in the ministry of the Holy Spirit because I want to speak in tongues." Sadly, these persons missed the point of the Spirit's main purpose in the lives of Christians.

Emotional lifts may be found in most of the pagan religions, or on a roller coaster, or in winning a contest. In themselves, they are not necessarily a sign of the Holy Spirit's working.

It is certainly true that the Holy Spirit does bring joy. Religious emotion is valid, but it is not basic. In our prayers we sometimes give more attention to blessings than to the Blesser. The primary function of the Spirit is not to bless us; his constant task is to bear witness to Christ (John 15:26), to enthrone Christ as supreme Lord (I Cor. 12:3).

As we spend time listening to God, the Holy Spirit will minister to our needs, leading us beyond symptoms to an understanding of causes and answers. Without the aid of the Holy Spirit, we are unable to find truth about ourselves or about God.

I remember having difficulty writing a term paper when I was in college. For two weeks I searched in the library for the proper materials. I found nothing, and the term was moving right along without my paper. Finally, I went apologetically to my professor and told him my problem. He explained to me in about thirty seconds just what I needed to know. Then he smiled and said, "Remember, young man, if you ever need help, don't be ashamed to ask for it."

The Holy Spirit is our teacher who says, "I'll show you what you need to know. I'll tell you what the right questions are, and I'll help you with the answers. Don't be ashamed to ask me."

At the end of our search for answers to our deepest problems stands Jesus Christ. He is not merely a help to the Christian life or just a supplement to it. Jesus *is* the Christian life. It is the work of the Holy Spirit to help us know this.

The Holy Spirit is our unseen ally. He speaks softly, but powerfully. He wants to communicate the life of Christ to each one of us. Through his ministry you can hear from God.

VII

Asking and Receiving

O God, Who art ever the same,
Let me know myself, let me know thee.

—St. Augustine

The great spiritual awakening that occurred in New Testament times brought salvation to many. For others, however, the ministry of Christ and the preaching of the apostles went unnoticed. The movement of God's Spirit had no effect on those whose eyes were closed to spiritual matters. They expected nothing, and they received nothing.

Even though the wind of God's Spirit is moving wonderfully in our own time, some remain unaware of it. But those with eyes to see realize that God is, indeed, actively working among us today, bringing new life and fresh hope.

Today, as in other times, human pride stands as the greatest obstacle to our receiving the blessings of God. In fact, one may fairly claim that man's pride in his own attainments is his most fundamental sin.

Some persons are afflicted with pride of possessions. They think that money and material holdings will bring human fulfillment. Such an attitude nourishes communism in other lands and materialism in our own land.

In many areas of American life the sole qualification for acceptance or success is the possession of money or some sort of material power. Such an attitude betrays the grossest sort of idolatry, an idolatry which cannot possibly satisfy man's deepest and most basic needs. Yet many persons, obsessed with perishables, persist in savagely dedicating themselves to achieving material conquests. Consequently, pride of possession has blinded them to their need of a power beyond themselves and to their own poverty of spirit. Paul described such persons accurately: "They think only of things that belong to this world" (Phil. 3:19, TEV). National leaders who emphasize political or military power as an ultimate goal or solution to man's problems are also victims of this same sort of pride.

Some who reject such downright materialism nevertheless succumb to a different sort of pride. For practical purposes we may call them humanists. For them, *learning* and *reason* constitute the ultimate goals in life. Humanism assumes that if men only know what is right, they will do it. Humanism appeals to man's reason, insisting that through rational thinking the conflicts within man and his world will be resolved.

The finality of human reason reigns as an unquestioned assumption on many university campuses and in the thinking of many sophisticated moderns. Although the good which reason has done is vast, reason has very definite limits. Man's finiteness and his innate sinfulness make reason an unsafe guide in seeking ultimate answers to life's questions.

While God is not *contrary* to reason, he most certainly is *above* reason. Nevertheless, multitudes of sincere persons look to reason for life's solutions, and some are even convinced that God and the transcendent realm of the Spirit may safely be relegated to ancient superstition.

There is one other area of pride even more sinister than the pride of material power or the pride of intellect—*spiritual* pride. Spiritual and religious pride feed man's ego, and this sort of pride is deadly because it blinds man to his continuous need of divine grace. The self-righteous Pharisees of Jesus' day remind us of the length to which spiritual pride can go. They thanked God daily that they were "not as other men," and gloried in their religiosity. "Religion," someone has said, "may well be humanity's final stronghold against God."

None of us likes to admit that he is unable to achieve worthiness before God in his own strength. Even Christians sometimes act as though the success of their spiritual life depends upon their own works instead of God. Until man surrenders his natural tendency to take pride in his moral achievements, the Holy Spirit can do little in his life.

God calls us to abandon all our pride—material, intellectual, and spiritual—so that he may come to us in the power of the Holy Spirit.

Often someone says, "I'd like to surrender my pride and experience the power of God in my life. How can I participate in a modern Pentecost of my own?" Three verbs provide an answer to this question: *come, ask, receive.* (1) *Come* to God in prayer. (2) *Ask* for the fullness of the Holy Spirit. (3) *Receive* God's working in your life by faith.

First, come to God in prayer. Prayer means, very simply, conversing with God. Prayer consists of opening our minds and our personalities to "dialogue" with our Creator. Talking with God should be as natural as talking with a friend. Prayer should be relaxed, not tense. Striving isn't necessary. After all, God is more willing to meet with us than we are to meet with him.

Christians do not pray in order to get a reward for saying their prayers. Jesus disapproved of certain of his contemporaries who prayed for this reason. Parading their piety in the open market place, they even printed prayers and wore them as badges on their robes. Jesus said that they were like "whitewashed tombs, which outwardly appear beautiful, but within they are full of dead men's bones and all uncleanness" (Matt. 23:27). Although outwardly respectable, they were inwardly corrupt. They prayed in order to *earn* the favor of God and man.

Christians pray because love prompts them to communicate with God. True prayer is not saying pious passwords to bring God to your side. Prayer is a heartfelt communion with God, and as we pray we participate in the life of Christ.

Some reject prayer as having little value for modern man. Recently, I heard a teacher of religion in a college insist that prayer could very well be eliminated from the life of the Christian. When asked why, he responded, "Prayer is only autosuggestion or self-hypnotism." Some

who would be shocked at such a bold denial of the value
of prayer actually pray very little. Habitually to neglect
prayer is but slightly less destructive than rejecting prayer
altogether. Our attitude toward prayer serves as a good
gauge of our attitude toward God.

Communion with God establishes the channel through
which God's vast resources can flow into our lives. A
general rule: the more we pray, the closer we draw to
God. The reverse is also true: the presence of God fades
as the practice of prayer declines.

Of course, the mere quantity of time spent in prayer
is not the key issue; the important consideration is the
quality and depth of the relationship with God which
results from spending time in his presence. John Calvin
was correct when he called prayer "the soul of faith."

Each promise of the New Testament which speaks of
receiving the Holy Spirit's fullness is linked with a sum-
mons to pray. Jesus himself often spent long periods in
prayer. He was such a man of prayer that his disciples,
praying men from their youth, said, "Lord, teach us to
pray." Prayer unfolds as a major theme throughout the
entire Bible; it is essential if we are to experience the
fullness of the Holy Spirit.

Sometimes when we come to God in prayer, we find
that we have sins that block communion. If this is the case,
our best recourse is to confess them. Scripture affirms
that God stands ready to forgive: "If we confess our sins,
he is faithful and just, and will forgive our sins and
cleanse us from all unrighteousness" (I John 1:9). Whatever obstacle you may face, don't be deterred; prayer

brings us into contact with the resurrected Lord. The first step in being filled with the Holy Spirit is to *come to God in prayer.*

Second, ask for the fullness of the Holy Spirit. James the apostle wrote, "Ye have not because ye ask not" (James 4:2, KJV). An international student once complained to me that a product he had purchased from a hardware store did not work. Plaintively he said, "I have tried for three weeks, and I just can't get this thing to operate."

I said, "The store is only two blocks from your dormitory. Have you asked the hardware salesman how it works?"

"No," he responded, "I never thought of that."

He could have avoided frustration if he had asked for help instead of just struggling along. In our lives we can escape a great deal of spiritual frustration if we come to God and ask him to meet specific needs.

I have observed at least four reasons why people fail to ask God for the fullness of the Holy Spirit. One is that they are unaware of the personal reality of the Holy Spirit; they think of the Holy Spirit only as a vague theological doctrine.

Paul passed through Ephesus and found some spiritually frustrated persons. He asked them, "Did you receive the Holy Spirit when you believed?"

"No," they replied, "we have never even heard that there is a Holy Spirit."

Apparently, they were ignorant of the gift of the Spirit which Christ had promised to the church; Pentecost was completely foreign to them. Unfortunately, numbers of contemporary church members remain unaware that they can be personally filled with the Holy Spirit. The absence of the Spirit's power in the lives of Christians accounts for much of the lack of spiritual dynamic in the church.

A radiant Christian woman in Cleveland, Ohio, said, "For sixteen years I was spiritually hungry. I was in church each Sunday, but I was hollow on the inside." She went on to say, "I asked my friends in the church, 'Isn't there something better for me?' Always, the answer was, 'Can't you ever be satisfied? You're as good a Christian as anyone in our church.' "

Then she brightened and said, "One day, I decided to pray directly to God about my emptiness and need. I asked God to fill me with his Spirit. He did so, and my spiritual hunger has finally been satisfied." Until her experience in prayer, the Holy Spirit was nothing more to this woman than a phrase in the Apostles' Creed. She represents many others like herself who ignore the Holy Spirit because they do not know about him.

Another reason some people do not ask God for the fullness of the Holy Spirit is that they want to live according to their own plans. Because they want to reserve the freedom to make their own decisions, they hesitate to invite the Holy Spirit to take charge of their lives. God's Spirit never forces himself on anyone; he works in us only when we invite him.

A minister talked with a young mother about what Christ could do in her life, explaining how to surrender totally to God. She said, "I don't mind being religious, but I don't want to carry my religion *that* far!" Total surrender to Christ was too radical a step for her at that time. But later she reversed her opinion, and today she has blossomed into a dynamic Christian woman.

Scripture speaks clearly at this point: complete surrender to Christ is necessary if we want the Holy Spirit's fullness. Our plans, our talents, and our priorities must be given to God if we really want God to invade our lives at a deep level. Peter points out that God gives his Spirit "to those who obey him" (Acts 5:32). We cannot insist on controlling our own lives and expect the Holy Spirit to work effectively in us.

Still another reason that some persons fail to ask God to fill them with the Holy Spirit is procrastination. They have every good intention of receiving God's fullness in their lives, but they busy themselves with other interests and postpone total commitment.

I once had dinner with a farmer in a southern state. After the meal, we strolled out to a lake which was located at the rear of his farm. The lake rippled with the activity of about two hundred mallard ducks. I asked him about them.

"Once while I was hunting up in the state of Tennessee," he said, "I discovered a nest of three duck eggs, and I just decided I'd bring them on home with me. My wife found the eggs in the pocket of my hunting jacket and asked me what I wanted her to do with them. I answered, 'I really don't know what to do. Why not put them under

a bantam hen?' " He turned to me, "They'll sit on anything, you know."

I nodded.

"Well, soon those eggs hatched out—I had one drake
and two ducks. They multiplied, and by the following
fall I had a nice little flock. Then the migration season
began, and my ducks became restless. I was afraid they
would fly off and I would lose them."

"So what did you do?"

"Each day for about two weeks I went out and threw
corn to them, and they got so excited that they forgot all
about migrating," he explained. "Those ducks are really
mine now; they're not about to fly away. Anyone in this
part of Georgia who wants a duck for dinner knows he's
free to get one here any time."

I began to think about my friend's story. Those ducks
allowed the free corn to supplant their inner urge to
migrate. The result of their procrastination was that they
became sitting ducks!

The New Testament records that a man once said
something like this to Jesus: "Sure, I'll follow you; but
later. First I must look at a field I just purchased." His
modern counterpart says: "Of course I want the Spirit
of Christ in my life. But first I want to get the house paid
off, and the kids through school."

God has put something deep within our hearts that is
more profound than the migrating instinct that he put
within those ducks. We possess what Pascal called "a
God-shaped vacuum" in our very nature. Even as those
ducks repressed their desire to migrate, we too sometimes

repress the tug of the Holy Spirit to be fulfilled in God.

One of the most important words in the New Testament is "today." We need to grasp something of the urgency of the "now" which runs throughout Scripture. God's offer to us is in the present, an offer so great that we dare not put off our response.

Another reason some persons fail to ask God to fill them with the Holy Spirit is fear. They are haunted by what people might say, panicky about what God might ask them to do.

Jesus told a parable about three men who received money and were told to invest it. Two men invested their sums and were rewarded. The third man said, *"I was afraid . . ."* His fear paralyzed his actions. His failure resulted in his losing everything that he had been given.

On the night Jesus was born, the first ones to hear the glad tidings were the shepherds. They were tending their sheep when a large company of angels burst into chorus. The shepherds were terrified! Luke's gospel says, "They were filled with fear." But the first words of the messenger of God were, "Be not afraid; for behold, I bring you good news of a great joy which will come to all the people" (Luke 2:9,10).

God's message consists of good news, news from which we need never shrink or be afraid. The Holy Spirit's presence will never make you a confused or fanatical person; his presence will lift you to your highest self. He will make you more fully human than you could ever be without him.

When Jesus met blind Bartimaeus on the road, he said

to him, "What do you want me to do for you?" Jesus was saying in effect, "Ask of me what you will; I want to meet your needs." Essentially, he is saying the same thing today. His attitude toward us is, "Ask me, and I will make you into a new person."

Our part is to ask, and Christ's part is to give. Thus, the second step for anyone wanting to experience a personal Pentecost is to *ask for the fullness of the Holy Spirit.*

Third, receive the Holy Spirit's working by faith. Receiving by faith is like taking a gift. The receiver of a gift does not earn it—otherwise, it is no longer a gift. Although we do not earn the presence of the Holy Spirit, we *do* have to reach out in faith and receive him. Faith means opening ourselves to God's working on our behalf.

A school superintendent said, "I don't know whether I can receive the fullness of the Holy Spirit—I do not deserve it." Of course he did not deserve it; no one does. God does not require worthiness, only willingness. When this school administrator began to see that God doesn't demand a righteousness which man is incapable of producing, he inwardly opened his life to Christ. As he did so, he was filled with a quiet joy.

We are more likely to stumble over God's promises because they are too simple than because they are too complex. We tend to complicate spiritual matters, but God's offer is always uncomplicated. As we open the door of our lives to welcome his coming, he comes in. The key which unlocks the door into God's presence is faith.

The distance between sight and faith is not as great as we sometimes think. Although Christian faith begins where sight ends, it is not a blind faith. It rests on a solid foundation—God's past actions in behalf of man. Christian faith is not a rash assumption; it is a certainty supported by the evidence of history. God's promises—both of judgment and of blessing—invariably work themselves out in the human family.

God remains all-powerful (he is able) and merciful (he is willing) in his relationships with man. He has promised specifically to come and dwell with all who put their trust in him. The book of Hebrews develops the idea that God approves and blesses those who place their faith in him, and in the famous "faith chapter" (11) the inspired writer gives numerous examples. The Christian has every confidence that what God has done in the past he will do in the future. Faith completes the trend of available evidence.

God cannot bless an apprehensive fearfulness that balks at belief, but he wonderfully rewards a confident faith that dares to enter into a trusting relationship with Christ. Lack of faith on our part develops not so much because we *cannot* believe his promises, but because we *choose* not to believe them. Faith trusts that God exists and that he rewards those who seek him (Heb. 11:6).

True faith involves letting Christ into every area of your life and placing all you have at his disposal. A pastor said with enthusiasm, "Our church provides a generous fund to help those with emergency needs. In my work when I see such needs, I have the resources to help. Because the church has given much, I can do much."

When we place what we have at Christ's disposal, he

works creatively with what we give him. The more of ourselves we give to God, the more he can do in our lives. Total surrender brings total blessing. So, the final step for anyone wanting to experience a modern Pentecost is to *receive the fullness of the Holy Spirit by faith.*

I once visited Flint, Michigan where a company official took me through the Buick automobile assembly line. I watched the fenders and the grilles descend upon the steadily moving frames. At one point in our tour, I sensed an excitement in my friend. He became more animated as we reached the place where the workmen start the motors. When one of the engines ignited, my friend proudly exclaimed, "You have just seen a new Buick come to life."

So it is with us. The Holy Spirit is the Spirit of life. We can have all the external accessories; but not until the Holy Spirit comes in his fullness to ignite our total personality do any of us fully begin to experience life. When the Holy Spirit invades us at the deepest level of our being, we really begin to function as God intended.

God offers us full participation in the adventure and romance of Spirit-filled living. The condition for receiving is our asking. Through the Holy Spirit God calls us to walk with Christ, and through the Spirit he has promised us everything we need for the journey.

VIII

The Holy Spirit and You

God dwells wherever man lets him in.
—Martin Buber

Modern technology has produced many wonders, but nothing ever invented can compare with the miracle of an ordinary man who is living in the power of God's Spirit. Although the great machines of our age are impressive, *changed persons* remain the greatest marvel of all. Victorious Christians provide the best possible demonstration of the validity of the Christian message. Such persons speak volumes by their very lives.

Vital Christian living does not belong to the one who is strong enough to conquer sin. It belongs to the one who in his weakness has learned to draw upon the resources of Christ. Paul the apostle possessed the kind of spiritual life that is available to each one of us. He testified, "I have strength for anything through him who gives me power" (Phil. 4:13, NEB).

In this chapter we shall look at what it means to be Spirit-filled and what the fullness of the Holy Spirit can mean in your life.

The fullness of the Holy Spirit produces at least four changes in our lives. (1) The Holy Spirit makes us more aware of Christ, (2) The Holy Spirit accelerates spiritual growth, (3) The Holy Spirit provides a new power, and (4) The Holy Spirit imparts a greater love.

First, the Holy Spirit makes us more aware of Christ. A sign of spiritual maturity is the deepening sense of living one's life in Christ. Paul, for example, said, "For to me to live is Christ" (Phil. 1:21). A sure sign of spiritual immaturity is a preoccupation with religious concerns while at the same time neglecting Christ.

Christianity that is truly vital focuses foremost upon the person of Jesus Christ himself. Many people in the church need to fall deeply in love with Jesus. They are like Peter when he "followed Christ afar off." A Spirit-filled Roman Catholic said, "For years I was what I thought a good Christian ought to be. I supported the church with my presence and my money. But religion was for me more a matter of duty than devotion because I had only a secondhand relationship with Christ." He went on to say, "The Lord has loved me all the time, but now I'm beginning to love him back."

Jesus said of the Holy Spirit: "He will glorify me, for he will take what is mine and declare it to you" (John 16:14). As important as the Holy Spirit is, we ought not to center our attention upon him. To do so is to open ourselves to a highly subjective kind of religious experience and to miss the point of his ministry.

Of course, I'm not suggesting that the Holy Spirit has a lesser status than Christ. Father, Son, and Spirit are equal members of the Holy Trinity. But I am saying that the Holy Spirit has a different *function* and *ministry*. The Holy Spirit seeks to direct our love toward Christ.

The New Testament does not admonish us to become like the Holy Spirit; we are urged to become *Christlike* in character. The Holy Spirit provides the dynamic, but the goal of the Christian is to grow "in the Lord" (Col. 3:9,10). Paul prays that "Christ be formed in you" (Gal. 4:19).

Technically speaking, since the Holy Spirit is fully divine, there is no reason why we could not pray to him. Yet prayers to the Holy Spirit have been rare in the history of Christian worship. And when we look at the Bible, we find that the Holy Spirit is the inspirer of prayer, but never the object of prayer. There are New Testament references to prayer *in* the Spirit, but no passage records prayer *to* the Spirit.

Spirit-filled New Testament Christians worshiped *Christ*. Their earliest and most basic creed was: "Jesus is Lord!" They reverenced the risen Lord, and they reflected his holiness in their lives. The Holy Spirit continues the same ministry of exalting Christ among us in our own time. Where the Holy Spirit is most active, Jesus Christ becomes most prominent.

Second, the Holy Spirit accelerates spiritual growth. An important part of the work of the Holy Spirit is to produce Christian graces or the fruit of the Spirit. In fact, the biblical writers place a greater stress on the moral and ethical results of the Spirit's indwelling than on any other aspect of his working. In the New Testament, solid Christian character receives far greater emphasis than miracles and special manifestations of the Holy Spirit.

Jesus said, "By this my Father is glorified, that you bear much fruit, and so prove to be my disciples" (John 15:8). Paul, under divine inspiration, outlines the fruit of the Spirit in Galatians 5:22,23. These graces are *love, joy, peace, patience, kindness, goodness, faithfulness, gentleness,* and *self-control.* All nine are moral virtues, pertaining primarily to our attitudes and our character.

The New Testament never suggests that Christians exhibit only *some* of the fruit of the Spirit. Quite the contrary! The New Testament writers tell us that God wills for every Christian to manifest *all* the fruit of the Spirit. The reason is simple: the fruit of the Spirit is rooted in the Holy Spirit, and where the Spirit dwells, his fruit is to be found.

In the passage on Spiritual fruit quoted above, the word *fruit* appears in the singular. The fruit of the Spirit compares to a rainbow. A ray of sunshine, when refracted through a prism, appears as several different colors. But the rainbow of color is merely a different way of viewing the original ray of sunshine. For purposes of analysis we may speak of red, yellow, green, etc. But in actual fact, these colors are all in a single ray of sunshine.

In order to let sunlight into a room, we don't say, "Today, I'll manufacture red light; tomorrow, I'll purchase some yellow light; later, I'll try to borrow some green light. Then, if I put them all together, I'll have sunshine." Rather, we simply draw aside the drapes and the morning sunlight floods into the room, a free gift from a loving creator.

In a similar manner, the fruit of the Spirit consists of various graces: love, joy, peace, etc. When the Holy Spirit works in our lives, he manifests himself in the full complement of his spiritual fruit.

In manifesting the fruit of the Spirit, we don't say, "Today, I'll work on love; tomorrow, I must try to produce some joy; later, I'll concentrate on peace . . ." Rather, the fruit of the Spirit results from God's spiritual sunshine, the Holy Spirit. When the Spirit dwells in our hearts, he begins to produce the fruit of the Spirit in our lives.

Of course, the fruit of the Spirit may be small and immature at first because we are such imperfect vessels. The fruit of the Holy Spirit requires growth, nurture, and cultivation. In fact, a large part of Christian maturation is the development of the Spirit's fruit. The fruit may begin to appear in a moment of time, but it matures over an entire life span.

Many Christians struggle to produce the fruit of the Spirit. But the fruit of the Spirit cannot be conjured up through hard work or diligent effort. Neither can it be counterfeited or produced by human will. The fruit of the Spirit is exactly that—it is the *Spirit's* fruit. Not your fruit, or my fruit, or the fruit of the church. The Spirit alone produces spiritual fruit, as we allow him to work in us.

Because Jesus loves his disciples, he does what is necessary to produce fruit in their lives. "I am the vine, you are the branches," said Jesus. "He who abides in me, and I in him, he it is that bears much fruit, for apart from me you can do nothing. Every branch of mine that bears no fruit, he takes away, and every branch that does bear fruit he prunes, that it may bear more fruit" (John 15:5,2).

Naturally, we sometimes chafe under Christ's discipline. The writer of Hebrews offers us this encouragement: "Now obviously no 'chastening' seems pleasant at the time: it is in fact most unpleasant. Yet when it is all over we can see that it has quietly produced the fruit of real goodness in the characters of those who have accepted it in the right spirit" (Heb. 12:11, Phillips).

The fruit of the Spirit is not a *condition* of receiving the fullness of the Holy Spirit; it is a *result* of his presence. When the Spirit operates freely in your life, you will experience an accelerated growth in spiritual graces.

Third, the fullness of the Holy Spirit provides a new power. Many Christians confess: "The spirit is willing, but the flesh is weak." Of course we are weak! And the sooner we admit it the better. Spiritual powerlessness can be overcome only through the working of the Holy Spirit within. "For it is God who is at work within you, giving you the will and the power to achieve his purpose" (Phil. 2:13, Phillips).

A grocer in a small southern village said, "I've tried hard to be a Christian, but I can't gain any victory over myself. I am so disheartened that sometimes I think I'll just quit." A forty-two-year-old minister of a large congregation in a state capitol said, "I can't go on much longer. Unless I can get free from my inner tensions,

I'm going to have to leave the ministry." Perhaps these persons were speaking your very sentiments.

Many Christians who have been made spiritually *alive* by Christ are not yet spiritually *adequate* in Christ. Certainly Christ is able and willing to empower us for meeting life's demands. But our busy and prayerless lives often *quench* the Spirit; our carrying the burden of unconfessed sin *grieves* the Spirit; and our self-will *resists* the Spirit.

Does God still love Christians who have walked more in the flesh than in the Spirit? Of course he does! Will he cleanse those areas of busy barrenness, unrepented sins, and self-will? Surely! Can he take the disordered and prayerless life of a Christian and fill him with the Holy Spirit in a fresh anointing, so that he can begin to rise above his circumstances? Absolutely! Moment by moment, he stands at the door and knocks, offering to lift us into a new dimension of life in the Spirit.

Jesus promised, "You shall receive power when the Holy Spirit has come upon you" (Acts 1:8). Paul emphasizes that the gospel consists of the Holy Spirit and power (I Thess. 1:5). John declares, "He who is in you [the Holy Spirit] is greater than he who is in the world" (I John 4:4). These verses represent the many biblical promises of power through Christ's Spirit.

The power provided by the Spirit enables us to serve Christ in true freedom. Spirit-filled Christians obey Christ not because they *must* do so, but because they are *enabled* to do so. A college professor said, "For me, the Christian life used to be a job—now it's a joy." The Holy Spirit changed his relationship to Christ from one of legalistic slavery to one of loving service.

The Holy Spirit also wants to give Christians his spiritual gifts. The gifts of the Spirit transcend natural talent and natural endowments. All persons have talents; but spiritual gifts go beyond mere human abilities.

The gifts of the Spirit are discussed in Romans 12, Ephesians 4, and I Corinthians 12. God intends us to have these gifts in the church today. Although no single Christian will possess all the gifts of the Spirit listed in the New Testament (I Cor. 12:4-11, 29-30), every Christian should exercise at least one or more of them (I Cor. 12:7,11).

The church will fail to function properly unless the gifts of the Holy Spirit are rediscovered and allowed their proper place in the church. If we seek to do God's work without the gifts of the Holy Spirit, we will be frustrated in our efforts to serve him.

In the church today we seem to have two equally unfortunate points of view with respect to the gifts of the Holy Spirit. In describing what I mean, I want to coin two words: *charisphobia* and *charismania. Charis* is a Greek noun which means "favor, gift, or grace." From this Greek word we get a currently popular word, "charismatic."

Christians who have charisphobia look with disfavor on the gifts of the Spirit. These Christians are afraid of fanaticism, and they are concerned with dignity and order in the church. The sort of fear I'm talking about is represented by Bishop Butler in the eighteenth century.

In a letter to John Wesley, he wrote: "Sir, the pretending to extraordinary revelations and gifts of the Holy Ghost is a horrid thing, a very horrid thing." Some contemporary Christians believe that the gifts of the Holy Spirit were strictly limited to the New Testament times, and they have no place in the life of the church today.

There seems to be, however, no biblical or theological reason why we ought not experience the gifts of the Holy Spirit in our time. Indeed, in a number of Christian circles the spiritual gifts *are* in operation! Paul's advice still stands: "Desire spiritual gifts" and "Neglect not the gift which is in thee" (I Cor. 14:1 and I Tim. 4:14, KJV).

Persons with charisphobia hinder the Holy Spirit because they do not *expect* him to work miraculously in and through them. Their fear of fanaticism blocks this significant aspect of the Holy Spirit's ministry in the church.

Other Christians have charismania. These Christians seem obsessed with the gifts of the Spirit, especially some of the more spectacular ones such as speaking with tongues. Throughout the history of the church there have always been those who sought to cultivate dramatic manifestations of the Holy Spirit. For instance, in Luther's day certain Christians became obsessed with direct revelations from God, and they went to ridiculous extremes in their emphasis on the Holy Spirit. Some said that the Spirit gave them permission to marry more than one wife; some set dates for Christ's return; and a number received private revelations that contradicted the Bible. Speaking of them, Luther quipped, "They swallow the Holy Ghost, feathers and all!"

Those with charismania sometimes ignore the biblical teaching that the Holy Spirit apportions his gifts to Christians at his own discretion (I Cor. 12:11,12). These Christians insist on telling God *which* gifts to give them and *when* to do so.

Sometimes these Christians root their beliefs in *experience* instead of Scripture. The mistake here is that some seek to universalize their own spiritual experiences, and insist that other Christians must have experiences like their own. They look to some of the *descriptive passages* in Acts as a basis for their beliefs instead of the *teaching passages* in the Gospels and the Epistles.

Another mistake sometimes made by those with charismania is the stressing of the *gifts* of the Spirit to the neglect of the *fruit* of the Spirit. Perhaps even more serious is the tendency at times to neglect the gift-giver because of a preoccupation with his gifts.

Unfortunately, those afflicted with charisphobia look down on those with charismania as "fanatics and disturbers of the peace." And those with charismania look down on those with charisphobia as "not spiritual" or as being "void of any knowledge of God."

The unity of the church is threatened by such extremes. Either an underemphasis or an overemphasis on spiritual gifts will undermine a wholesome balance in the church.

As I see it, the plain truth is this: God wants to use all Christians by giving each one a spiritual gift (or a cluster of gifts) so that the church may be fully equipped for its ministry in our world. At the same time, he wants to be free to distribute the gifts of the Spirit among Christians as he sees fit. Certainly, without the gifts of the Spirit the church will not be able to minister in the power of the Spirit.

The gifts of the Holy Spirit illustrate the sort of power that results from the fullness of God's Spirit. The significant fact is that God wants to do mighty things in and through the lives of Christians in our time.

The fullness of the Spirit brings a new power for us *to be* and for us *to do*. Truly, "if any one is in Christ, he is a new creation" (II Cor. 5:17). Thomas Chalmers called the work of Christ's Spirit "the expulsive power of a new affection." The inner presence of the Holy Spirit results in a power which is not our own—a power that scatters the night of mediocrity and ushers in the dawn of vital creativity.

Fourth, through the fullness of the Holy Spirit, we begin to love others in a new way. Beyond any question, love stands as the supreme sign of God's working in our lives. Yet, few of us love others as we should. Estrangements are all too common among Christians. Broken relationships and our general lack of concern about human need can be overcome only through love. Paul summarized the importance of love when he counseled: "Love is the fulfilling of the law" (Rom. 13:10).

Many of us are far too preoccupied with ourselves and therefore not really free to love. We tend to become resentful when someone threatens our self-esteem. When we feel our "rights" have been violated, we are ready to defend ourselves. We sometimes quarrel in the church—even over the Holy Spirit! Our disunity certainly doesn't stem from the Holy Spirit; it comes from our lack of love.

The Holy Spirit, however, can conquer our unloving attitudes by imparting to us a measure of God's love. When we begin to see ourselves loved and affirmed by God, we no longer have to defend our "rights." We can rest securely in God's love and be free to love others in Christ. Jesus has said, "By this all men will know that you are my disciples, if you have love for one another" (John 13:35).

The Holy Spirit does not make us better than others, but he does make us better than we were before we allowed him to have full control of our lives. The gift of God's love to us leaves no room for human pride, for it is entirely the work of grace: "Let us go on loving one another, for love comes from God" (I John 4:7, Phillips).

Is it difficult to be filled with the Holy Spirit? Not if you're really sincere. God does not ask us to beg and plead. The Holy Spirit is already trying in countless ways to make himself real in our lives. And even when we close one door to our inner self, he seeks admittance through another. All God requires is that we respond to him, that we open our lives to him in complete surrender.

In a retreat, a middle-aged housewife and part-time secretary in a university said, "My Christian life has been a disappointment to me and to others who have had to live and work with me. I was converted to Christ twenty-two years ago, and people know I'm a professing Christian. But I've spent most of my Christian life worrying and fretting, and I'm a pretty bad advertisement for Jesus. Christ has forgiven me, but I surely don't display very much Christlikeness in my life."

The retreat leader asked her if she surrendered herself daily to Christ and if she regularly prayed for Christ's help. She replied, "No, I've pretty much tried to do it all in my own strength. But as I've listened to the witness given by others at this retreat, I'm beginning to see that Christ doesn't expect *me* to live the Christian life. He wants to live his life through me."

The leader suggested, "It's never too late to start over."

After more conversation, she prayed, "Lord, all I am and all I have I lay out before you on this table. I'm not proud of my life. But such as it is, I surrender it to you. Fill me with your Holy Spirit and cleanse me from worrying and fretting. Help me to rely on you from now on. I can't live another day without your power."

Later she said, "I feel as if Christ has freed me from the burden of self-effort. I know the Holy Spirit has come to me in a new way. From now on I'm going to trust Christ instead of relying on myself."

Essentially the New Testament teaches, "Whatever your need may be, surrender that need to Christ." Do not merely analyze your problem; surrender it.

Once one of our children appeared at breakfast, not up to his usual vigor. I sensed that he was not feeling well, but I asked, "Son, what can I pass you? Would you like eggs, or cereal, toast, or what?"

He was looking pale and excused himself saying, "I

don't want anything, Dad. I feel just awful. I'm going back to bed."

In two days the same scene was reenacted, except that his normal good health had returned. Once more I asked him what he wanted me to pass him. This time his eyes lit up and he said, "Pass me some of everything on the table, and I believe I want two helpings."

This enthusiasm pleased me—certainly every parent loves to provide for healthy and responsive children. Then I thought of a Scripture passage: "If you then, who are evil, know how to give good gifts to your children, how much more will the heavenly Father give the Holy Spirit to those who ask him!" (Luke 11:13).

The results of Spirit-filled living will probably be the greatest surprise you have ever experienced. Paul writes that by the Spirit's power we are "able to do infinitely more than we ever dare to ask or imagine" (Eph. 3:20, Phillips).

The Holy Spirit is more than a doctrine; he is more than a substitute for the risen Christ. He is the mediator of Christ's living presence to each one of us.

As we remain open to him, he works creatively in our human personalities to reshape us after the pattern of Christ! He sanctifies and redirects our natural abilities. Through his working we receive his remarkable gifts and graces. And by his indwelling, he lifts us into a new dimension of living which Christ described as the abundant life.

IX

Freedom Now

Freedom is the capacity to counteract statistics.
—Antoine de Saint-Exupéry

Embedded within every human heart is an innate desire for freedom. Men will go to great lengths to obtain freedom—freedom of speech, freedom from poverty, freedom from war. But we can achieve freedom in all these areas and still not have freedom of the spirit. Spiritual freedom may be found only in Jesus Christ. "If the Son makes you free, you will be free indeed" (John 8:36).

The freedom which Jesus came to give is freedom for the whole person. Jesus began his public ministry with these words about freedom:

The Spirit of the Lord is upon me
because he has anointed me to preach good news to the poor.
He has sent me to proclaim release to the captives
and recovering of sight to the blind,
to set at liberty those who are oppressed,
to proclaim the acceptable year of the Lord (Luke 4:18-19).

We usually think of freedom as something we have to earn through hard struggle. With some kinds of freedom this is true. But freedom in the realm of the human spirit is a gift of God. It is not something we win by sweat; it is something we receive by grace.

In this final chapter we will examine spiritual freedom in terms of what it can mean to you. The Holy Spirit brings inner freedom in four areas. He gives us freedom from *self*, freedom from *sin*, freedom from *sanctions*, and freedom from *society*.

First, the Holy Spirit brings freedom from self. Many Christians are not really free from themselves. A high-ranking military officer reported: "I command several thousand men, and they fear and obey me; but I cannot command my own will."

A construction worker in his mid-twenties said, "I want to be different than I am, but I can't." Both men were in the same dilemma. They wanted to change themselves, but were unable because they were bound within. Man can control the atom, but he cannot control himself.

No amount of camouflage or mask-wearing can conceal our failure to handle ourselves. Once, I was driving to a speaking engagement, my family along with me. When almost there, I was flustered to discover that I had forgotten my notes. One of my children, then six, said, "Daddy, why don't you put some pieces of typing paper on the pulpit? You can pretend that you have your notes, and no one will know the difference."

But people *do* know the difference. Role-playing does not convince anyone for very long. Phoniness has a way of seeping through our cleverest attempts to hide it.

One of the paradoxes of the Christian faith is that

freedom from self comes only with surrender of the self. When self is surrendered to God, the Holy Spirit frees it to realize its highest potential. The Holy Spirit works in us in a way which unfolds as a continuing miracle. Self-surrender to Christ results in self-mastery through the Holy Spirit. George Matheson captured this thought in a splendid way:

> Make me a captive, Lord,
> And then I shall be free;
> Force me to render up my sword,
> And I shall conqueror be.

We are not able to control all our external circumstances because we have no way of preventing many of the things which occur in our lives. But we can receive God's help so that we are freed from fear and enabled to meet whatever comes our way. True freedom finds its source in Christ, and it results in an inner happiness that is quite independent of outer circumstances.

We become emancipated when we become properly related to Christ. "Whoever seeks to save his life will lose it; and whoever loses it [in Christ] will save it, and live" (Luke 17:33, NEB).

Second, the Holy Spirit brings freedom from sin. Many persons find themselves sinning, not always because they want to, but because they cannot help it. Time and again, they vow that they will stop that sin only to find themselves right back in the same old rut. They hate their sin, but cannot liberate themselves from its grasp.

A sincere Christian housewife said, "Most of the time

I do fairly well in my Christian life. But I have this 'besetting sin' which I just can't seem to shake." Her experience was not unusual; many Christians can identify with her.

To be bound by any sin speaks of our lack of freedom. Paul taught, "If you put yourselves at the disposal of a master, to obey him, you are slaves of the master whom you obey; and this is true whether you serve sin, with death as its result; or obedience, with righteousness as its result" (Rom. 6:16, NEB). When you are unable to resist steady tempation, you obviously are not enjoying the Christian liberty that God has in store for you.

The good news of the Christian gospel is that Christ can both forgive your sin and liberate you from its tyranny. He offers a better way of living than our repeating the cycle of sinning and repenting over and over. The prophecy given to Joseph before Jesus' birth underscores this thought: "You shall call his name Jesus, for he will save his people from their sins" (Matt. 1:21).

Most of us are tempted to yield to two kinds of sins: outward sins and inward sins. These may be described as the hot-blooded sins of the flesh and the cold-blooded sins of the spirit. Although the subtle sins of disposition may be unseen, they are as damaging to our relationship with God as are the more obvious outward sins. For instance, one may refrain from murder or adultery, while harboring inward hate or lust.

Christians, however, do not have to live in servitude to sin. Writing to the believers at Rome, Paul observes, "Thanks be to God, that you who were once slaves of sin have . . . been set free from sin" (Rom. 6:17,18).

Of course, perfection of performance belongs to Christ alone. Because of imperfect understanding and human limitations, Christians cannot function with the perfection of the angels. For this reason all Christians need regularly to pray the "Lord's Prayer," which includes a phrase concerning forgiveness (Luke 11:4). The best Christians stand continuously in need of divine grace.

However, Spirit-filled Christians can experience freedom from a regular pattern of *willful* sin. In a letter to first-century Christians, John included the following statement: "In writing thus to you my purpose is that you should not commit sin" (I John 2:1, NEB). The verb *should not commit* is in the present tense and can be translated, *you should not continue the practice of habitual sinning.*

We can sum up the matter this way: We all fall short of absolute perfection of *performance,* but the Holy Spirit can give us pure *motives.*

No one ever experiences God's deliverance apart from his presence. We ought not to think of God's power apart from his person. The Holy Spirit is more than the *giver* of power; he *is* the power.

The book of Acts contains an account of a man named Simon, a magician who had the ability to amaze people with his sorcery. Being greatly impressed by the miracles done through Philip, a Christian evangelist, Simon requested Christian baptism, with the hope that he too might be enabled to perform such miracles. He coveted the power of the apostles and even offered to pay money if they would pray for him to receive the Holy Spirit. He was denied the Holy Spirit because he wanted the power of the Spirit only for personal aggrandizement. He wanted to perform spectacular feats, but he had no interest in the Spirit's sovereignty over him. Simon wanted the results of the Spirit working in his life without any personal relationship with God.

Although we cannot have the results of God's presence apart from his person, we can have *both* if we are willing. Through fellowship with Christ, the Christian finds freedom from the domination and tyranny of sin. "Where the Spirit of the Lord is, there is freedom" (II Cor. 3:17).

Third, the Holy Spirit brings freedom from sanctions. God intends Christians to live above the negative strictures of rules and regulations. Martin Luther described it this way: "Christians live under grace, not law."

I sat with another minister at a banquet where I was to give the invocation, and he was to pronounce the benediction. We ministers flanked the honored guest of the evening, who was not a Christian. During the meal he turned to the other minister and asked, "What is a Christian?"

The other minister responded with these words: "You want to know what it means to be a Christian, do you?" His eyes narrowed, and he continued, "Well, Christians don't smoke, they don't drink, they don't gamble, and they don't curse."

To my way of thinking, his answer was utterly inadequate. It was entirely negative, consisting of no good news. It was based on *law,* not *grace.* The minister had failed to mention forgiveness, new life, freedom, or Christ. Christians do not live by negatives, but by positives.

When the Christian gospel is presented as a series of "dos" and "do nots," it is not surprising that some persons lose interest in the church. They may not be rejecting Christ at all. More likely they are rejecting a legalistic perversion of the gospel. To add *anything* of human merit to the gospel is to misread the New Testament.

In Paul's day, there were teachers who insisted that non-Jews had to submit to circumcision before they could be Christians. Paul strongly repudiated the addition of any regulation as a prerequisite for saving faith. He wrote to the Galatian Christians urging, "For freedom Christ has set us free; stand fast therefore, and do not submit . . . to a yoke of slavery" (Gal. 5:1). Paul is saying in effect, "Rejoice in God's gift of salvation; you are free from the shackles of slavery and the burden of having to earn God's favor by a plodding obedience to legalistic prescriptions."

Since the Christian life is not based on rules and regulations, what are we to make of the commandments found in the Bible? Are we to ignore them? Relegate them to the dark ages? Not at all! The law holds an important place in the life of a Christian.

The main function of the law in the Christian life is to give *moral direction*. Augustine's famous dictum, "Love God and do as you please," needs some qualification. Such an approach to Christian living demands a well-educated conscience.

In ourselves, we lack the wisdom to know what to

do in life's situations. We need to be biblically informed as to what pleases God and what doesn't. This is where the law comes in. The law makes clear God's will for us; it points to the life-style which God wants us to follow.

An illustration of what I'm talking about is found in the fifth chapter of Paul's letter to the Galatians. In that chapter Paul discusses walking in the Spirit and walking in the flesh. In order to leave no doubt about what it means to walk in the flesh, he writes, "Now the works of the flesh are plain" (Gal. 5:19). Then he lists fifteen specific actions *forbidden to the Christian*. These works of the flesh are off limits, not so that the Christian *may* be saved, but because he *is* saved.

Then Paul writes about walking in the Spirit. He tells specifically what fruits the Spirit-filled person will have in his life (Gal. 5:22-26). Paul writes not to *threaten* the Christians, but to *inform* and *inspire* them.

While Christians are free from the demands of legalism in religion, they are not free from the demands of love. And the demands of love exceed the requirements of any set of rules. This is what Jesus meant when he said, "I tell you, unless your righteousness exceeds that of the scribes and Pharisees, you will never enter the kingdom of heaven" (Matt. 5:20).

In the story of the good Samaritan, the priest and the Levite passed by on the other side of the wounded man. The law did not *require* them to stop and help. But the demands of love compelled the good Samaritan to stop, bind up the injured man's wounds, and care for him.

Jesus said that the sum total of God's requirements is found in love—love to God and love to neighbor.

Granted, there is always the possiblity that the gospel of grace will be perverted into an excuse for a careless disregard of the law. Throughout Christian history, there have been those who have perverted the gospel of grace to the extent that they justified sinning with reckless abandon. Such action violates the nature of Christian liberty. To those who were seeking to use grace as an excuse for sin, Paul wrote, "Shall we sin to our heart's content and see how far we can exploit the grace of God? What a ghastly thought! We, who have died to sin—how could we live in sin a moment longer?'" (Rom. 6:1,2, Phillips).

Christian liberty is not the freedom to do anything which pops into one's mind. It is freedom from the iron fist of the law; it is the liberty to realize one's full potential as a child of God.

Fourth, the Holy Spirit brings freedom from society. You are not really free until you are free from the opinions of others. Many persons lack freedom because they are intimidated by what people around them think and say. H. G. Wells once said, "The voice of our neighbors sounds louder in our ears than the voice of God." Whenever we permit others to determine our course of action, we are not really free persons.

Some people resist society's pressure to conform, yet they still lack true freedom. They overreact to others. In seeking to avoid the influence of the world, such persons gravitate into a tiny spiritual clique and live in a religious

126

ghetto. In an effort to preserve their spirituality, these people retreat from any obligations they may have to their surrounding culture. Although well-intentioned, they have not found true freedom any more than those who allow themselves to be squeezed into the world's molds.

True freedom is never achieved by withdrawing from responsibilities and from the pressures common to our life in the world. Such freedom is a negative freedom, often characterized by pride. Withdrawal from involvement in the turmoil of life is too simplistic a solution to the problem of dealing with social pressures.

Real freedom does not mean being swept along in the current of contemporary culture, nor does it mean crawling out of the river and resting on the bank. Rather, true liberty consists of making progress against the stream and overcoming the current. One is truly free when he can live victoriously in the midst of the gritty problems of life. Real freedom neither acquiesces to the shallow opinions of others, nor shrinks from responsibility and challenge.

God sets the Christian free so that he may develop fully in Christ, and so that he may constructively channel his energies toward the good of others. The presence of the Holy Spirit fortifies us to go into the world and live redemptively as children of God.

Look with me at one of the freest men who ever lived: Paul, the apostle. He belonged exclusively to Jesus Christ, and the power of the Spirit surged through his personality. His was a liberated soul bound to nothing but God.

He was content in plenty and in poverty. He knew how

to live in the midst of success and plenty and how to cope with failure and want. He possessed a serene calmness whether he stood before kings or sat in a jail.

He was free enough to go against the opinions of other Christians when he believed they were wrong. Yet, he willingly submitted to the "weaker brother" rather than cause him to stumble. Paul was an adequate man because he was filled with the Holy Spirit.

Yet Paul was completely human—no different from you and me. He was no plaster saint. He got discouraged, had temptations, suffered indigestion, and was bothered by chronic eye trouble that God did not heal. But Paul was a free man because he was free in Christ.

Christ's promises of freedom are as valid for us as they were for Paul. God wants us to have freedom now! And as we have seen, spiritual freedom results from a radical commitment to Jesus Christ as Lord which brings a total openness to the working of the Holy Spirit.

In Christ, you can meet life with confidence because he lives in your heart. You are liberated to reach your highest potential through the power of Christ's indwelling Spirit. You are free to embrace life fully because you know that nothing can separate you from his love.

In your Christian liberty your life will take on a growing splendor. As you adventure more deeply into the life of the Spirit, you will find increasing joy and unimagined fulfillment. You're free, because you're free within. And this freedom belongs to you forever. You know to whom you belong, and you have confidence that he guides you unfailingly into a glorious future.